Basic Techniques in Data Communications

Basic
Techniques in Data
Communications

Ralph Glasgal

Artech House

Copyright © 1977

ARTECH HOUSE, INC.
610 Washington Street
Dedham, Massachusetts 02026

Printed and bound in the United States of America.

All rights reserved. No part of this book may be repro-
duced or utilized in any form or by any means, electronic or mechanical, including photocopying, recording,
or by any information storage and retrieval system,
without permission in writing from the publisher.

Library of Congress Catalog Card Number: 77-18090

Standard Book Number: 0-89006-057-6

Dedication

I had intended that my earlier book would be my last, but now that this volume is completed, I am sure I mean it. Thus, this is my final chance to write a dedication that will long survive the book, at least in the hearts of the dedicatees.

To Scarlatti, our cat, who regularly incubated the manuscript;

to my parents, in-laws, and other relatives, who have skeptically tolerated my neglect of them for the years it has taken me to produce the books;

to my daughter Kim, who perfected her typing skills on the typescript;

to my wife Linda, who, like Penelope, tactfully undid my daughter's typing every night;

to my daughter Rana, who fortunately was too young at the time to want to type the manuscript;

and finally, to my loyal customers in the New York metropolitan area, whose moral and financial support saves me from having to make a living as an author —

I dedicate this book with gratitude.

Foreword

With every day that passes, the need for swift, accurate digital data communications becomes more of a necessity in keeping the government and industry of a densely-populated, modern civilization functioning efficiently. Without the near-instantaneous availability via communication of such things as account balances, inventory status, stock prices, currency rates, and seat or room occupancy, to list just a few, our present economic system would quickly falter and our civilization would drift into disorder. Non-electronic methods of data transfer, such as mail, or analog methods, such as telephone conversations, are no longer adequate to sustain the economic activity of a modern industrial nation. There is every expectation that the growth in digital communications will accelerate, and that a sort of digital society eventually will evolve, in which private homes are equipped with two-way digital terminals receiving digitized television, music, news, credit, and messages broadcast from space stations.

In this book, the focus of the discussion is on the present-day, sophisticated hardware required to implement many different types of data communications links. After a brief investigation of fundamentals (which more knowledgeable readers may wish to skip over), an in-depth discussion of short- and long-haul data transmission using various types of drivers and modems is provided. Following are details about equipment that can be used to configure and control systems, and to diagnose specific network problems. The book concludes with a coverage of some devices that enhance the usefulness and versatility of modems. Other advanced systems equipment, such as multiplexers, concentrators, wideband interfaces, and other topics, are discussed in the author's preceding, complementary volume, Advanced Techniques in Data Communications, *also published by Artech House.*

July 1977   *Ralph Glasgal*
                                            Old Tappan, New Jersey

Table of Contents

Basic Techniques in Data Communications

1

Baudy Bits

The Basics of Data Communications

A very basic data communications system is shown in Figure 1-1. Data to be transmitted is put into digital format by the source, presented to the interface, sent via the communications medium, received by the remote interface, and interpreted by the sink. Typical data sources that format or store data are teletypes, printers, cathode ray tube terminals, paper and magnetic tapes, disks, punched cards, and computers. Interface units (which convert the digital source data to a format suitable for transmission) include line drivers, modulators, modems, radio transmitters, microwave dishes, loudspeakers, flashlights, and even Boy Scouts using semaphore. The most common data communications medium is, of course, the telephone or telegraph line, but light beams, sound waves, and radio waves are also perfectly acceptable media. The remote interface is the receiver; it interprets and restores the data to a digital format that the sink can interpret. The most common data sink is a computer.

Bits vs. Bauds

Bits are the units of binary digital information. Bits may be combined to form characters, and characters may be grouped to form blocks. A bit of binary digital data may be a 1 or a 0 — no other state is possible. In contrast, the baud is the unit of signaling. One baud is the shortest signaling element in a given transmission channel. Signaling elements sometimes are restricted to 1 or 0 states (referred to as marks or spaces),

Figure 1-1/The Basic Elements of a Point-to-Point Data Communications Link

1

but quite often signaling elements may have several positive or negative values other than 1 or 0. A baud may represent more or less than one bit in a given transmission system. For instance, if we say that two blinks of red light mean a 1 and two blinks of blue light are a 0, it takes two baud (blinks) to transmit one bit. On the other hand, if we say that one blink of red light means 00, one blink of blue light means 11, one blink of yellow light means 01, and one blink of green light means 10, then it takes only one baud (blink) to transmit two bits.

In this book we try to use the term "baud" when we mean the rate at which the transmission of signal elements is occurring, and "bits per second" when we refer to the amount of data passing through a channel.

Asynchronous Data Transmission

All data transmission is clocked in some manner and therefore is synchronous in a sense. However, for purposes of definition in this book, synchronous data is data found in systems in which all clocks are identical in rate over a long period of time. Thus, synchronous data is clocked out of the source at the same average rate it is clocked into the sink. How data clocks are kept synchronized over vast distances is discussed in Chapter 5. By contrast, in asynchronous transmission, the clock that clocks data from the source is nominally independent of the clock that clocks the received data into the sink. Obviously the two clocks must be related in some manner, or the data would be garbled. In most systems, the send and receive asynchronous data clocks originate in oscillators that generate clocks accurate to within approximately 1% of one another. If both clocks could be started simultaneously, they would remain in reasonable synchronism for many bits before the drift between them became noticeable. Indeed, since data bits almost always are grouped together to form characters, it is best to restart the oscillators each time a character is transmitted — which is what actually is done.

2

It is easy to synchronize transmitted data to a transmit clock since a data bit can be sent each time the clock cycles. At the receiving end, the problem is more difficult. Since an idle line in a binary system is by definition in the marking state, how do you detect the beginning of a character if its first baud is a mark? The answer is to preface each character with a non-data bit called a start bit (actually a start baud). The start bit is always a space, and its function is to tell the receiver that a character is starting. The transition from mark to space starts the receiver's clock and allows the receiver to count out the bits in the character. If the receiver oscillator is reasonably accurate and if the character is not too long, no timing errors occur. Thus asynchronous transmission essentially is accomplished one character at a time.

Suppose now that asynchronous characters are being sent continuously, without pause, and that the last bit of a character is a space. There then would be no mark-to-space transition between the end of one character and the start bit of the next to mark the moment at which the receive clock should be restarted to count out the next character. Therefore it is necessary to guarantee a minimum period of marking between asynchronous characters. This marking period is the rest or stop interval and is measured in rest bits or stop bits.

The start and stop bits limit the efficiency of asynchronous data transmission since, if a character has eight data bits, at least ten bits must be transmitted. In terms of signaling elements (baud) and information elements (bits), ten baud must be signaled for every eight bits of information transmitted.

Synchronous Data Transmission

Because of the inefficiency of asynchronous data transmission and the upper bound of about 1800 baud for asynchronous data transmission via phone lines (see Chapter 4), synchronous data transmission has come into widespread use. Synchronous transmission proceeds without start or stop

bits and, instead of single characters, large blocks of characters can be transmitted without pause. In synchronous data
transmission, a transmit clock sends out data to a receiver
which clocks in the data at an identical rate; all bit intervals
are equal, including idle bit intervals between blocks of data.
Nevertheless, even synchronous data transmission has characteristics which lead to inefficiencies and which must be
taken into account if a full understanding of synchronous
systems is to be had.

The blocking of data in serial synchronous transmission systems is not just optional, it is mandatory in practical systems.
First, each block of data must be prefaced with one or more
synchronization characters so that the receiver can identify
which groups of bits in the stream are characters. Remember
that in the synchronous case there are no start bits to locate
the first bit of a character for the receiver. The blocks also
must be of finite size so that the receiver can periodically
check its synchronization and recover from clock "glitches"
or timing errors due to noise, Doppler shift, modem errors,
etc. In essence, the synchronization characters and the idle
characters between blocks constitute a more efficient form
of the start and stop bits that were needed in asynchronous
transmission. Other characters in synchronous transmission,
such as "Start of Header," "Start of Text," "End of Text,"
"End of Transmission," and block error checks, are required
to ensure that blocks of data are received in order and without error. Many block transmission protocols have been developed by the major computer manufacturers and, unfortunately, there is not the same standardization in this area as
there has been in asynchronous data transmission.

Communication Links

While light blinkers, smoke signals, and drums were used in
the past to transmit data characters, copper wire and microwave beams are the mainstays of today's data transmission
systems, with optical fibers coming on strong. The most uni-

4

versal communications link for data is, of course, the switched or dial network, which was constructed originally for voice communication. Other examples of switched networks, however, such as Telex, TWX, and some specialized carrier networks, were designed specifically for data or for facsimile transmission.

For those who must transmit a lot of data to the same location, a private or leased line is desirable. Such lines may be analog or digital; two-wire or four-wire (see below); narrowband, voiceband, or wideband; and via satellite or terrestrial links. The properties of these different offerings are discussed in the following chapters of this book.

Full Duplex and Half Duplex

All elements in a data communications system can be defined in terms of their abilities to send and receive sequentially or simultaneously. A device or phone line that can only receive or only transmit is called simplex. Television networks are examples of simplex communications systems — TV sets are simplex receivers, TV cameras are simplex transmitters, and TV broadcast networks are simplex transmission media. By contrast, when you make a *local* phone call, it is possible to both speak and listen simultaneously or alternately. The former is called a full-duplex conversation, and it is difficult for most humans and data terminals as well. An alternating conversation is called half-duplex and usually is easier for persons and machines.

In brief, a full-duplex (FDX) device or line can send and receive simultaneously while a half-duplex (HDX) device or line can send and receive, but not simultaneously. In practice, applying these definitions is not as simple as it may seem. Terminals, modems, and lines each may be FDX or HDX. If an HDX terminal is used with FDX modem and line, the resulting system is still basically HDX. A modem that operates FDX on an FDX line may need to operate HDX on an FDX line to accommodate an HDX terminal. A line that is HDX

5

with one type of modem may be capable of FDX operation with another. In the chapters that follow, these anomalies are explained.

In the case of the dial-up and leased lines with which we primarily are concerned here, we can define the common line offerings in terms of whether they are FDX or HDX. The four-wire leased line consists of a send pair and a receive pair; since these pairs are completely independent, four-wire lines are inherently full duplex, even if they are used with half-duplex modems or terminals. Two-wire leased lines are inherently half-duplex; their bandwidth, however, can be split to form what amounts to two or more channels, as in frequency-division multiplexing or with some low-speed modems. Similarly, two-wire dial network connections are inherently half-duplex unless frequency-division multiplexing techniques are used.

Echo Suppression

Two-wire dial network connections can be used only for FDX communication using multiplexing if the line has no echo suppressor. An echo suppressor is a switchable attenuator used on long-distance phone lines to prevent an echo on the line from confusing a speaker with a delayed replica of the speaker's own voice. The echo attenuator or suppressor switches rapidly in direction as each speaker becomes a listener. Therefore, this type of long-distance voice call is a half-duplex call. For HDX data calls, it is desirable to disable the echo suppressor since data signals often do not properly reverse the echo suppressor circuits which were, after all, designed to be triggered by speech; also, the reversing process is a slow one. The echo suppressors can be disabled by transmitting a single tone in the band 2000 to 2250 for slightly less than half a second. Once disabled, the echo suppressor remains disabled for the duration of the call, unless the signal on the line drops out for more than 50 ms. It should be mentioned that modems are designed to cope with the echoes

6

that remain on the line once the suppressors are disabled. For FDX data calls, disabling the echo suppressors is mandatory since transmission must be possible in both directions simultaneously.

Line Conditioning

Phone lines are prone to such impairments as noise, distortion, and frequency translation, described in detail in Chapter 8. Some line impairments can be controlled on leased lines by means of special networks. Such arrangements are called "line conditioning" and the phone company offers several different types to control frequency response, phase response, signal-to-noise ratio, and harmonic distortion.

C1, C2, and C4 conditionings represent increasing degrees of perfection in regard to bandwidth and delay. Another form of conditioning, D1 (D2 for multipoint lines), guarantees a signal-to-noise ratio better than 28 dB, a second harmonic distortion down 35 dB, and a third harmonic distortion down 40 dB below the signal level. C2 conditioning is often required by modems operating at 9600 bps; it guarantees a frequency response of 300 to 3000 Hz + 2 dB, -6 dB and a difference in delay between 500 and 2800 Hz of less than 3 ms. By contrast, a C1 line has an upper limit of 2700 Hz; a C4 line, 3200 Hz. C3 conditioning is reserved for access lines and trunks in switching centers, and usually is not a factor in data transmission.

EIA RS-232 Interface

An entire book could be written on the ramifications of the Electronic Industries Association (EIA) specification RS-232, which governs the interface between data terminal equipment and data communications equipment. In this introductory chapter, we try to show why the signals in this interface are necessary and how they relate to the modes of transmission (HDX, FDX, Async, Sync, two-wire, four-wire, and dial-up).

There are two parts to RS-232 — one specifies the electrical characteristics of the signals crossing the interface; the other governs the connector pin numbers and the functions of these signals. The electrical characteristics are summarized briefly below. The interface signals may be either positive or negative, with an absolute voltage of 3 to 25 V. Signals between +3 and -3 V are not defined. If a signal is data, a mark is defined as negative voltage and a space is defined as positive. If the line is a control signal, the function is on when the voltage is positive and off when it is negative. In synchronous interfaces, the negative heading edges of clock signals correspond to the centers of the data bits. The interface lines are not damaged if accidentially shorted to ground or to each other, and the recommended load impedance is 3000 to 7000 Ω. The EIA interface is nominally limited to cable runs of up to 50 ft and to data rates not exceeding 20,000 bps. A female 25 pin connector is mounted on equipment such as a modem; a cable that ends in a male connector usually is furnished with terminal equipment.

Note that in the following figures, if a signal is an output from a modem, it must be an input to a terminal. A definition implicit in the specification is the meaning of Receive Data and Send Data. In a modem, Receive Data (pin 3) is that data which the modem is receiving from the telephone line and demodulating, not what it is receiving from the terminal. Similarly, Transmit or Send Data (pin 2) is what the modem is transmitting down the telephone line. From the terminal's point of view, receive data is what it receives from the modem; transmit or send data is what it wishes to transmit.

Leased Line System Control Signals

In the simplest system, shown in Figure 1-2, all elements are full duplex. In a full-duplex system, the only EIA signals required are Data and Carrier Detect. An active Carrier Detect signal is required in virtually all systems to allow the terminal

8

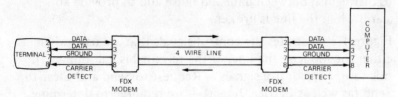

Figure 1-2/EIA Signals Needed in a Point-to-Point Full Duplex System

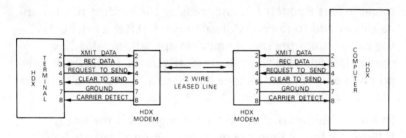

Figure 1-3/EIA Signals Needed in a Half Duplex Point-to-Point System

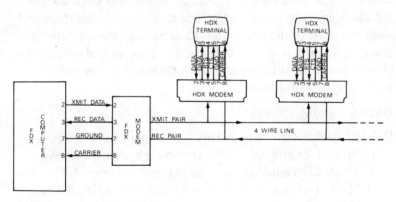

Figure 1-4/EIA Signals Needed in a 4-Wire Multipoint Polling System

9

to distinguish between data and noise and to provide an alarm when the line is broken.

Figure 1-3 illustrates the control signals that are used when either the modem, the line, or the terminal is half-duplex. In this case, two control signals — Request to Send and Clear to Send (as well as Carrier Detect) — are required to determine the direction of transmission. The first terminal that wishes to transmit raises Request to Send. After a delay to allow the modems to send and detect the carrier, the modem tells the terminal if it is clear to send. After transmission, the terminal lowers Request to Send, causing the modem to turn off its carrier and to lower its Clear to Send. After a brief delay, the carrier from the remote modem appears, heralded by Carrier Detect; data from the remote terminal follows. In this point-to-point system, Request to Send is raised by a terminal only if Carrier Detect is off.

In the multipoint polling system of Figure 1-4 the line is full-duplex but the remote modems and terminals are half-duplex. The central site polls the remote terminals by sending an address character. The terminal so addressed then replies by raising Request to Send. Since the central site modem needs to send its signal to all locations and since the line is full-duplex, the central site modem operates full-duplex and does not need to use the RTS-CTS protocol. Thus, carrier is always on at the remote locations, but goes on and off at the central site as each terminal in turn responds to the poll by sending carrier and data.

Dial-Up Control Signals

Dial network systems are usually half-duplex (unless frequency multiplexed) and are categorized by whether they answer or originate calls automatically or manually. Figure 1-5 shows the EIA control signals needed in a manually controlled system. There is essentially no difference between this system and the one of Figure 1-3. The call is dialed manually and, when the other end answers, both operators transfer control

10

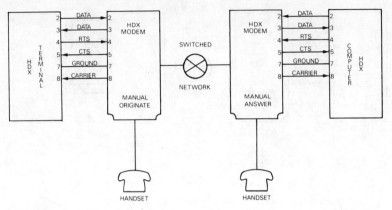

Figure 1-5/EIA Signals Used in a Manually Operated Dial Network System

to the modem. The modem then raises Data Set Ready to indicate to the terminal or computer that it is now in the data mode. The call is terminated manually at both ends and Data Set Ready drops.

When one end is unattended, the modem must answer and hang up automatically. Several additional control signals therefore are necessary, as shown in Figure 1-6. After manual dialing is complete, the phone at the remote end rings. The modem detects the ring voltage on the line and generates the EIA control signal, Ring Indicator. The computer responds with Data Terminal Ready if it wishes to answer the call. Upon receipt of Data Terminal Ready, the modem goes off-hook and sends an answer tone to the originating end. This tone has two main functions — telling the caller that a data set has been reached and, if the call is long distance, disabling the echo suppressor. The auto-answering modem raises Data Set Ready, indicating that a call has been answered and, in some cases, that the answer tone period is over. The computer then either may wait to receive data or raise Request to Send if it initiates transmission. At the end of the call, the computer lowers Data Terminal Ready to cause the modem

11

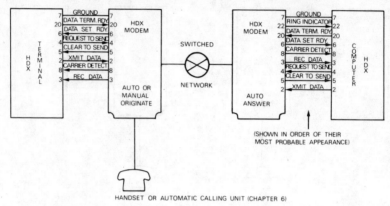

*Figure 1-6/EIA Signals Used in the Auto Answer Dial
Network Configuration*

to hang up. Other disconnect methods are also possible and
are discussed in a later chapter.

Finally, Figure 1-6 also shows a system in which calls both are
originated and answered automatically. At the originate end,
Data Set Ready comes on as soon as the automatic calling
unit has detected an answer tone and transferred the line to
the modem. Data Terminal Ready must come on at this time
or the modem will hang up.

While Ring Indicator, Data Set Ready, and Data Terminal
Ready have significant functions only in switched network
systems, they often must be biased on if switched network
modems are used on private lines or switched network computer ports are attached to leased-line modems.

Other EIA control signals and clock leads are discussed in
Chapters 4 and 5. Additional information on EIA interface
signals and the new EIA RS-XYZ interface, DDS, and wideband interfaces is given in the author's *Advanced Techniques
in Data Communications.*

2

The
Short Haul

Limited Distance Data Transmission

Normally, remote terminals are connected to their corresponding computer ports via modems and phone lines. Indeed, communicating terminals are specifically designed to be connected to modems; even if these terminals happen to be located only a few feet from a computer, some ingenuity therefore may be required to avoid using modems while making the terminal and the computer think they are connected through a pair of them.

In this chapter we discuss the many ways in which terminal equipment can be interconnected without modems over distances of less than a few feet to several miles. We consider such devices as no-modems, low-capacitance cables, line drivers, limited-distance modems, modem eliminators, and optical links. Each device described solves two problems. The first is to match electrically the terminal's digital EIA output to the type of transmission line involved; the second is to look like a modem and to furnish a terminal with the control signals and clocks it requires.

The First 100 Feet

The EIA RS-232 interface specification says that EIA interface cables should not exceed fifty feet in length for data rates up to 19,200 bps. While there have been cases where poorly designed RS-232 transmitters and receivers have been unable to operate over even 25 ft of cable, most experts would agree that cable lengths up to one or two hundred feet often can be used for data rates up to 1800 bps without ill effect. The exact length that can work in a particular case depends on the capacitances of the cable leads to ground and to each other, the output and input impedances of the driver and receiver, the data rate, and the magnetic or electrostatic noise level in the immediate vicinity of the cable. Unfortunately, no hard-and-fast rule can be given. But as a first resort for data rates up to 9600 bps at distances up to one hundred feet, one should try a simple EIA extension cable.

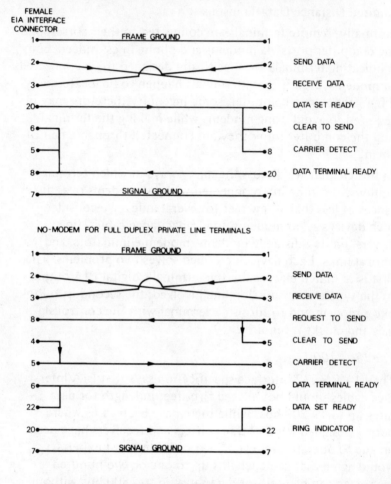

Figure 2-1/No-Modem Cable Adapters for Asynchronous Terminals or Computers.

Connecting a terminal to an asynchronous or synchronous modem or multiplexer via an EIA cable is usually a very simple matter, requiring only a cable of the proper length with a

16

male connector at the modem end and either a male or female at the terminal. In cases when a computer comes equipped with a cable, the cable ends in a male connector. Therefore, if an extension cord is needed, it must have a female connector at one end and a male connector at the other. The female connector must be equipped with lock nuts so that the male connector's screws can be used to fasten them together.

Directly interconnecting two modem-seeking terminals, such as a terminal and a computer, is quite a different matter. A simple extension cord does not suffice since, in this case, the terminals must be fooled into thinking they are connected to modems and the sexes of the connectors must be matched. In the asynchronous case, either a specially wired cable or a terminal box (sometimes called a no-modem or a null-modem) is required. Figure 2-1 shows how to wire no-modems for a full duplex terminal and a switched network half-duplex terminal. The no-modem essentially is twist-wired so that output signals reach input lines and each terminal sees the proper EIA control signal voltages. Although not illustrated, no-modems for terminals with reverse channels are also possible, and other cross-connection combinations often work just as well as the ones shown. The types shown have the advantage of not requiring any power supply voltage on either pin 9 or 10. In cases in which a computer is polling several local terminals, the extension cable with a no-modem cannot be used. Instead, a device variously called a line-sharing unit, a multiple-access unit, a modem-sharing unit, or a contention unit can be employed economically. Such devices have multiple no-modems built into them and contain switching to connect the computer with the terminal that answers the poll. Contention devices such as these are discussed in greater detail in the author's *Advanced Techniques in Data Communications.*

Synchronous terminals also can be interconnected via EIA RS-232 extension cables, if a no-modem containing a clock

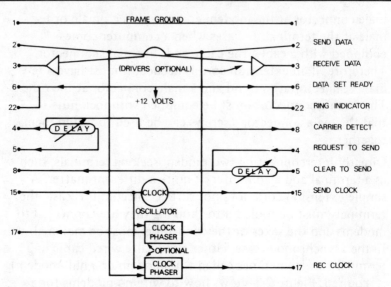

Figure 2-2/A Modem Eliminator Interconnects Synchronous Terminals.

is provided. Such a device most often is called a modem eliminator. The modem eliminator shown in Figure 2-2 provides send and receive clocks to both terminals, but otherwise resembles the asynchronous twisted cable adapter. Since power is available in the no-modem, it is possible to add such options as Variable Request to Send, Clear to Send Delay, and Receive Clock gated off by Carrier Detect. Note that only one modem eliminator is required to replace two synchronous modems. Figure 2-3 shows how a modem eliminator can be used with a modem-sharing device to configure a synchronous polling system. Terminals in this system usually can be up to 200 ft from the computer, since the line-sharing unit regenerates all signals in both directions.

18

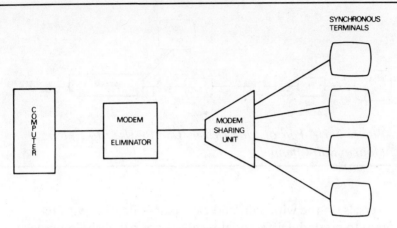

SYNCHRONOUS
TERMINALS

COMPUTER

MODEM
ELIMINATOR

MODEM
SHARING
UNIT

Figure 2-3/A Modem Eliminator Used with a Modem Sharing Unit Interconnects Local Polled Synchronous Terminals.

Stretching to 500 Feet with Extended Data Cables

Now on the market is an EIA-type cable with such properties that it can be used over distances five to ten times greater than those possible with conventional cable. Such cable is constructed to have less capacitance and is shielded; it has been used at 9600 bps on runs of 500 ft without difficulty and is certainly an extremely simple, cost-effective, and reliable approach to the short-haul problem. This cable does have a larger outside diameter than the standard cable; therefore, an eighteen-lead version, which has a diameter that fits well within the standard EIA connector shell, is sometimes used. Extended data cables can be used directly or wired as no-modems in any of the configurations illustrated above.

Line Driver Approach

For asynchronous data transmission over distances of several thousand feet, a line driver is a practical approach. A line driver works by converting the bipolar EIA signal to a low-impedance, balanced signal suitable for long-distance transmission via twisted wire pairs. Data is represented by polarity

19

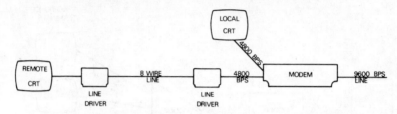

Figure 2-4/A Pair of Line Drivers Can Be Used to Extend a Modem Sub-Channel.

reversals on the wire pair, and each pair is floating with respect to ground. Differential receivers are relatively immune to noise and crosstalk, and it is possible in this manner to transmit data up to five miles at 1200 bps or one-and-a-half miles at 9600 bps.

Since line drivers do not modulate or encode data, they require dc continuity. They also require one pair of lines for each data or clock line transmitted. Thus, four wires are the minimum needed for send and receive data. Line drivers also are used for synchronous data but, in this case, eight wires are required to accommodate receive and transmit clocks. Many line drivers do not generate clocks; thus, synchronous line drivers are used mostly to extend a port of a multichannel modem or multiplexer. Such an application is shown in Figure 2-4.

Control signals can be generated locally by the line drivers, but not all line drivers can detect the presence or absence of carrier. In many applications this limitation is not significant. However, if line drivers are used in a polling configuration with a line-sharing unit, the Request to Send signal from each of the polled terminals must be carried on a separate pair to the line-sharing unit; alternatively, the line driver can transmit such control signals as changes in dc potential between send and receive pairs or between the send and receive pairs and ground. In general, line drivers are inexpensive and reliable, but are usually less cost-effective in synchronous data or multipoint applications.

Limited Distance Data Encoders

One function of the standard long-haul modem is to convert digital data to a form compatible with leased or dial-up phone lines. This transformation includes eliminating any dc component and compressing the bandwidth to fit in the 400 to 3000 Hz region of the average phone line. Other functions of most modems include the ability to turn carrier on or off — thus providing an additional slow-speed data transmission channel — and — in the case of synchronous modems — the ability to generate and transmit data clocks. All of which is accomplished by standard modems on four-wire private lines at speeds up to 9600 bps. A limited-distance modem (or, more properly, data encoder) can accomplish these ends more economically if the lines involved are only a few miles in length and free of critical line impairments such as frequency translation (see next chapter).

For asynchronous data transmission up to 300 baud, the best approach for any distance over 500 ft is still the standard 103-type modem. A private line modem costs very little, is available from many sources, can operate on a single two-wire line, can be used in multidrop polling configurations (since it can detect and control carrier), and does not require line response down to dc. For asynchronous rates between 300 and 1800 baud, a four-wire 202 modem is the best choice and the most economical where dc continuity is not available. The 202 also can be used easily in multidrop systems (as is discussed in later chapters). For asynchronous speeds over 1800 baud, the line driver is the most practical approach, but lines with dc continuity are required; above 4800 bps, more than the usual leased-line bandwidth is required. Synchronous limited-distance data encoders do not have the above disadvantages and, if used in conjunction with the in-

21

expensive asynchronous-to-synchronous converter units, they can transmit 7200 or 9600 bps asynchronous data over distances of several miles at little expense.

It is much easier to design inexpensive synchronous short-haul adaptors for use on short four-wire, ac-coupled, normal-bandwidth leased lines than to design asynchronous adapters; the use of a clock makes it possible to use data-encoding or translation techniques that eliminate the dc component of binary data streams and reduce the required line bandwidth. The normal binary data present at the EIA interfaces of terminals or computers technically is categorized as a polar Non-Return-to-Zero waveform (NRZ). In the EIA RS-232 NRZ data format, a mark is defined as a negative voltage and a space as a positive voltage. Consecutive marks or spaces result in continuous negative or positive voltages; therefore, an NRZ data stream has much energy at or close to dc.

Fortunately, there are many ways to transform synchronous NRZ data so as to eliminate the dc component without resorting to modulation. Since we are dealing with synchronous data and sometimes with multidrop networks, the methods we describe must feature clock recovery, four-wire operation, and pseudo-carrier control features. Simple data scrambling is not an ideal solution to this problem, although its deficiencies are of interest here. NRZ can be scrambled by mixing it with a known repetitive pseudo-random data stream or key. By this means, any long periods of marking or spacing are eliminated and the dc component therefore is essentially eliminated. In addition, enough data transitions occur to keep a receive-data clock recovery circuit operating properly.

Scramblers and descramblers must be synchronized to each other, however, and this synchronization takes time. Thus, in a polling system, the polling time would be lengthened significantly as the master unit synchronized itself to each incoming scrambled data stream. Other drawbacks include mul-

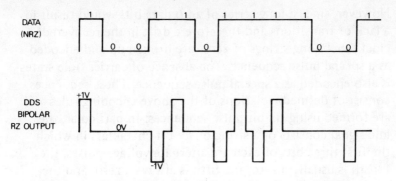

Figure 2-5/Data Encoding Scheme Used in Bell DDS Network.

tiplication of errors when synchronization is lost and the lack of a simple means of carrier signal control.

The two most common short-haul transmission techniques are the one used by the Bell System to provide local loops for their Digital Data System (DDS) network and the one commonly employed by modem manufacturers in their short-haul product lines. In the DDS network, a Data Service Unit (DSU) is provided instead of a synchronous modem as the interface unit between a customer's terminal equipment and the DDS network. The DSU is essentially a type of lim-ited-distance data encoder that operates over 4-wire ac-cou-pled lines, providing clock recovery and pseudo-carrier con-trol. Incoming NRZ data is converted to the outgoing bipolar return to a zero signal according to the following rules — if the data bit is a zero, the voltage is zero for the entire bit period; if the data bit is a one, a pulse with a width of one-half the bit period is generated. The polarity of these pulses alternates for consecutive 1's (see Figure 2-5). The alteration of 1's in this manner insures that no dc component is gener-ated. The data clock is recovered from the receive data stream by synchronizing a local flywheel oscillator to receive data transitions.

However, since a long series of zero data bits would result in a lack of transitions and therefore a drift in the recovered clock, such long strings of zeros are broken up and encoded as a special pulse sequence. The absence of carrier (idle states) is also encoded as a special pulse sequence. These sequences consist of defined violations of the above encoding rules and are formed using six-bit pulse sequences. In particular, the idle signal consists of a string of six-bit characters in which the first three bits of each are alternate voltage pulses, the fourth is usually a zero, the fifth is always a zero, and the sixth is a pulse the polarity of which violates the rule that consecutive pulses must alternate polarity. A dc component does not develop when consecutive idle characters are sent since the odd number of bits in the first three positions assures that the polarity of the sixth pulse, although wrong, alternates, thereby eliminating any dc bias. The fourth bit of the first character of an idle period occasionally can be a pulse of either polarity, due to the fact that when the line went idle an odd pulse might just have been transmitted.

In a similar manner, long strings of zeros are broken up into special characters called zero suppression sequences. These characters consist of zeros in the 1, 2, 3, and 5 positions. The sixth bit is always a pulse of the wrong polarity, and the fourth bit is a zero or a pulse of either polarity as required to keep a dc bias from developing. Other violation sequences are possible, but they are not available for use by the DDS subscriber. A pair of DSUs apart from the DDS network can be used as short-haul units, but a master transmit clock oscillator must be provided at at least one end. The coding technique used by the DSU has one major disadvantage — the pulse width is half the bit period, which means that the DSU signal requires twice the bandwidth of the unencoded data. While wideband lines can be provided to DDS customers, the ordinary leased line, even for the short haul, usually is loaded by the phone company with networks at the termination points.

24

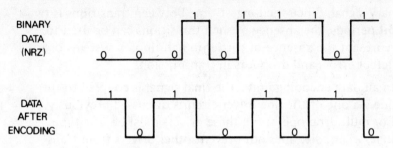

Figure 2-6/Delay Modulation Encoding Used in Most Limited Distance Modems Eliminates the dc Component of Binary Data.

The bandwidth therefore is limited enough to prevent this DDS encoding technique from being practical at 7200 or 9600 bps, and 4800 bps is marginal.

Fortunately, a phase encoding technique (sometimes called delay modulation) requires no more bandwidth than the original NRZ data, has a dc-free spectrum, and, since the longest possible time between transitions is two bits, always has edges to which a receive clock can be synchronized. It is this technique that has been used to build many of the synchronous four-wire line drivers on the market. As shown in Figure 2-6, consecutive zeros are represented by transitions at the end of a bit interval. Thus a string of zeros looks like a square wave with a frequency of half the bit rate. A string of ones is represented by a square wave at half the bit rate with transitions occurring in the middle of the bit period. When the data changes from zero to one, the transition that is normally at the end of the zero bit is delayed until the middle of the one bit. When the data changes from a one to a zero, no transition occurs until the end of the zero bit. If a single zero occurs between two one bits, no transition occurs between the midpoint of the first one bit and the midpoint of the second one bit. The simplicity of this technique is startling, considering its advantages. Compared to the DSU technique it has the advantage of being a true two-level bi-

25

nary signal. Since the longest time between transitions is two bit periods, the absence of such transitions can be used to represent the absence of carrier in half-duplex systems or to detect errors and dropouts in transmission.

In all data encoding units, the final signal is coupled to the line via one of the line driver circuits discussed previously. For multidrop operation, these drivers must be of a type that, when idle, does not prevent other drivers from transmitting.

Optical Line Drivers

One way to beat the exorbitant cost of short-haul wideband data transmission is to use a light beam. Infrared laser units are available that can transmit up to 250 kbps of data between tall buildings or across airfields, campuses, lakes, or rivers without requiring phone company or FCC approval. Data can be transmitted optically over distances about twice as far as the eye can see. While one might think that bad weather would be an insuperable problem, statistics have shown that, even in the worst meteorological parts of the United States, system availability is about 98%, which compares favorably with phone-line uptime. The optical equipment (with a channel multiplexer, if desired) costs less than a pair of 9600 bps or 50 kbps modems, and there is no monthly line charge.

3

Here Today, Gone Tomorrow

The Data Access Arrangement

There was a time, not so long ago, which we could call BC (Before Carterfone), when nothing but telephone-company-supplied equipment (modems, handsets, teletypes, switchboards, etc.) could be connected directly to the dial network. In the BC era, virtually the only way in the United States to get digital data onto a dial-up line, using non-Bell-supplied equipment, was to use an acoustic coupler. Many futile hours were spent by mechanical engineers trying to design contraptions with levers and arms that could automatically answer, hang up, or originate calls without making an electrical connection to the phone line.

This frustrating state of affairs was ended in late 1968 by a modern-day messiah named Carter, who persuaded the FCC to allow non-Bell equipment to be attached to the telephone network. But Carter's victory was not complete. In its wisdom, the FCC permitted the phone company to require and charge for a protective device (Data Access Arrangement or DAA) to be interposed between the dial phone line and any non-Bell equipment. No tariffed DAA was required for leased line circuits.

This period, AD (Anno DAAs), ended in the summer of 1976 when the FCC (and then an appeals court) decided that protective devices were not required after all for data devices the FCC certified as safe. The seven years of the AD period saw a tremendous growth in the number of non-Bell modems manufactured and attached to the dial network via Bell-furnished data access arrangements. Even though the DAAs nominally belong to history, it will be some time before they and the thousands of modems designed to operate with them pass into oblivion. Modem users now can buy and install DAAs made by independent manufacturers for use with their older equipment. Additionally, many of the DAA functions were essential and therefore must be duplicated in the new generation of certified modems. Therefore, an intimate knowledge of the soon-to-be-obsolete DAAs is of more than just historical interest.

29

Manual Data Access Arrangement

Data calls can be originated and answered manually or automatically. We first consider the simplest DAA, the CDT-1000A, which is used with a telephone handset to establish and answer data calls. The designations CDT, CBS, CBT, etc. have no special meaning and are simply telephone company order codes. Figure 3-1 shows an interconnection diagram of the CDT coupler. To make a data call, one simply picks up the handset, dials, and waits for the other end to answer. The exclusion key (the white button on the left side of the cradle) then is lifted to transfer the line from the handset to the modem. If the call is answered manually, the answering party must also lift its exclusion key to transmit data. The CDT unit has no options, takes its power from the phone line, and does little more than permit switching between data and voice; it also puts a voltage-limiting circuit between the phone line and the modem to prevent phone company circuits from being subjected to high signal levels that might cause interference to other subscribers.

As can be seen in the circuit diagram, the switchhook switch shunts the ringer and line when the handset is lifted. The line then can be transferred from the handset to the modem by

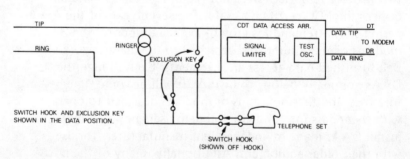

Figure 3-1/Connection Arrangement for CDT Manual Data

lifting the exclusion key. Note that the handset must be left off its cradle during data transmission. The handset cannot be used to monitor the local data transmission tone on the line; however, if the exclusion key is dropped, it is possible to hear a tone coming from the remote modem — a useful diagnostic factor. The DAA contains straps which are set by the installer so that the signal limiter in the DAA limits the signal from the modem whenever the signal level at the central office exceeds -12 dBm. The installer usually writes on the coupler the level at which the modem should be set so as to avoid activating the limiter, which probably would cause distortion and degrade performance. For example, if the line loss to the central office is 5 dB and the coupler loss is 2 dB, the maximum allowable modem level is -5 dBm (-12+5+2) — which is what should be shown on the coupler and what the modem should be set to output.

Automatic Answering DAAs (CBS and CBT)

The major reason for using either the CBS or CBT Automatic DAAs is that electronic answering of a phone call is desired. Apart from cost, the only significant difference between the CBS and CBT units is that the former presents an EIA RS-232 voltage interface to the modem, and the latter looks for and generates contact closures. Both the CBS and CBT units come in two models. The CBS-1001A unit was made more compact when it became the CBS-1001F but it is otherwise similar. The full part numbers of the CBT units are CBT-1001B and CBT-1001D.

The main function of a DAA in the automatic answering process is to detect when the phone is ringing and to translate the ringing signal to either a contact closure or EIA voltage. There are several other control signals required in this answering process; perhaps it is best to introduce them by describing their functions in answering a call. We assume that no handset is associated with the answering DAA.

31

When the line with an automatic DAA is called, the central office puts a ring signal on the line. The ring detector circuit in the DAA detects this signal and raises Ring Indicator (RI) to the modem. This signal normally passes through the modem to a computer which, if it wants to answer the call, raises Data Terminal Ready, which in turn causes the modem to raise the signals Off Hook (OH) and Data Transmission (DA) to the coupler. The OH signal causes the coupler to answer the call; its operation is equivalent to answering a call manually by picking up the handset. The DA lead causes the DAA to connect the modem analog signal tip and ring leads to the line via the signal-limiting circuit described in the CDT section above. The coupler response to the DA signal is not instantaneous, but rather is delayed by one to three seconds. The purpose of the delay is to prevent the modem from putting on the line at the moment of connection high frequency tones that would prevent the automatic billing devices from properly registering the completed call. When the delay is past, the DAA raises Coupler Cut Through (CCT) to tell the modem that data transmission can proceed. To terminate a call, the modem simply lowers OH.

Figure 3-2 is a functional block diagram of the CBS or CBT Data Access Arrangement, showing its connection to the line, modem, and optional handset. As with the CDT unit, the modem level must be set so that the signal at the central office is -12 dBm.

Automatic Call Origination with DAAs

Both the CBS and CBT Data Access Arrangements can be used to originate calls automatically in conjunction with an automatic calling unit. Pulsing the OH lead generates dial digits, or, if both the OH and DA leads are energized, the dialing tones can be transferred through the coupler to the line. Chapter 6, devoted to automatic calling units, contains details of such systems.

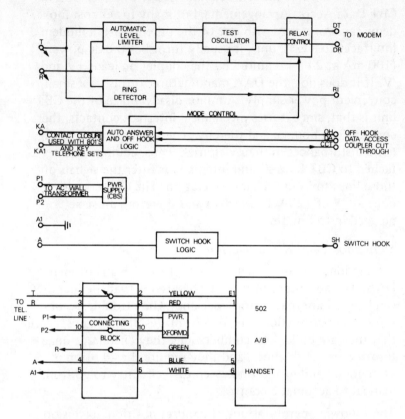

Figure 3-2/Block Diagram of Automatic Data Access Arrangement

Selecting the Proper DAA

Once a manual or an automatic DAA is assigned to each end of a system, a choice must be made between CBS and CBT units. In general, the CBT unit is to be preferred because it is the lowest cost device, particularly when it can be ordered without power supply. The choice of the unit really depends on the modems and/or automatic calling unit with which it will be used. Some modems can be used with either CBS or CBT Data Access Arrangements, but many lower cost modems can work only with one or the other. When a modem interfaces to a CBT unit, it usually furnishes the dc power (100 mA at 24 V) required by the coupler on leads +V and -V. If it does not, the DAA manufacturer furnishes a small, convenient power supply. A minor disadvantage of the CBT unit is that, since it uses mechanical interface contacts, these contacts can bounce and thereby generate small electromagnetic disturbances in their vicinities. Thus, equipment attached to CBT lines should integrate or filter the signals on those lines to insure reliable operation. The CBS coupler requires 8 W of 120 V power (ac) and therefore must be plugged in to function.

Switchhook and Ringer Options

A telephone handset usually is furnished with an automatic DAA. The advantage of having a handset is that the line then can be used alternately for voice and, when trouble occurs, for voice coordination. The disadvantages of the handsets are that they are bulky and cumbersome, they encourage unauthorized use of the lines, and they require the addition of switchhook and exclusion key control circuitry to go from manual to automatic control.

The following permutations of handset position, exclusion key position, and audible ringing are possible:

	Handset Position	Exclusion Key Position	Audible Ring	Auto Answer	Manual Originate	
	on-hook	down	yes	no	no	coupler controls line; ring
A	off-hook	down	yes	no	no	indication to coupler only
	off-hook	raised	no	yes	yes	
	on-hook	down	yes	briefly	no	coupler controls line, ring
B	off-hook	down	yes	briefly	no	indication to coupler and
	off-hook	down	no	yes	yes	telephone set
	on-hook	down	no	yes	no	telephone set controls line, ring
C	off-hook	down	no	—	yes	indication to telephone set or
	off-hook	raised	yes	no	no	coupler only
	on-hook	down	no	yes	no	telephone set controls line, ring
D	off-hook	down	no	—	yes	indication to telephone set or
	off-hook	raised	yes	briefly	no	to coupler and telephone set

In brief, A is the preferred arrangement. The A and B options allow the DAA to answer a call even with the handset in position on its cradle. Options C and D require that the handset be left off its cradle and the exclusion key be up for automatic answering of a call. Options A and B are much neater and there is no risk that the exclusion key has fallen down unobserved. Options A and C have the advantage of preserving quiet in installations where hundreds of calls a day may be answered automatically on many lines.

Loop Current Sensing Option

Bell system modems, being connected directly to the phone line, are able to monitor the dc current on the line to a central office. An interruption or reversal in line current of more than 5 ms after a call has been completed is usually an indication that the remote end has disconnected. In many systems this line-current-loss sensing capability is the only way a call can be terminated. Early DAAs did not provide for current monitoring, and so independent modems could not be used where alternate methods of disconnection — such as carrier loss disconnect (no good in half-duplex systems), long space disconnect (no good if line disconnects by accident), and abort timer (no good if carrier and RTS are off simultaneously) — were not available. Eventually a loop-current-sensing option was added to the Data Access Arrangements. It consists of a relay in series with the line, which turns off the switchhook or line current lead to the modem when the line current drops below 20 mA. Not all central offices interrupt line current when calls are disconnected, so this point should be checked before specifying this option; the modem also must have a provision for responding to this signal.

DAA Test Features

The CDT, CBS, and CBT couplers all contain a 2800 Hz oscillator for test purposes. When activated, the test button conditions the DAA for testing from a remote location, such as a central office. The DAA is called, and either an answer button is pressed or, in the newer units, if the test button is on, the unit automatically answers the call and puts the 2800 Hz tone on the line. The calling location then can measure line levels and the action of the automatic-level-control circuit.

CDH and Connecting Arrangements

Some users have non-Bell Private Branch Exchanges (PBXs) for voice communications. The trunk lines to these PBXs are usually ground start lines — lines in which dial tone is requested by grounding the ring side of the line until the central office responds with a ground on the tip side of the line as dial tone comes on. At night, when these trunk lines are not being used for voice, they can be used for data. A CDH connecting arrangement with a CBF option permits data transmission through the PBX or directly via the trunks. The CBF option is a signal-level limiter similar to that found in the CDT unit; the CDH unit is quite similar to the CBT.

Latest Interconnection Arrangements

As a result of the FCC decision referred to earlier, it has been permissible since August 1976 to connect equipment such as modems, automatic calling units, and data access arrangements directly to the line. The FCC decision is being implemented in two phases. In the first phase, it is possible to direct-connect equipment from manufacturers who made equipment for the independent telephone companies and such carriers as Western Union. This so-called grandfather approach puts manufacturers who have been serving their segments of the telephone industry on an even footing with Western Electric. Grandfathered units contain all the line-holding and ring-signal-detection circuitry required to connect directly to the tip and ring leads. The plugs and jacks described next for registered equipment may also be used with grandfathered equipment.

The second phase of the FCC's interconnection decision is the registration program. Manufacturers may submit equipment to the FCC for registration. Once registered, such equipment may be connected to the dial network via any of the FCC-prescribed plug-and-jack arrangements. The phone company will provide a standard jack upon request, if provided with the registration number of the equipment and the Ringer Equivalence Number of the registered unit. The Ringer Equivalence Number tells the phone company how much central office power and ringing current are required to support the device involved. For example: a typical key set, such as the 565, has an REN of 1.0A. A typical modem uses less current than a handset, since an audible ring is not generated, and its Ringer Equivalence is typically .4A or .6B. The "A" and "B" refer to the frequency range over which the equivalency is valid. A typical equivalency for a modem and handset together would be 1.4A.

The registration program provides three different approved ways to connect to the line. They all have the basic purpose of insuring that the signal arriving at the central office is not greater than -12 dBm, just as the DAA did. The first is the permissive arrangement. In this arrangement, the modem output is not adjustable but is fixed at the factory at -9 dBm. Since the loss to the central office is typically -3 dB, the -12 dBm level will be achieved most of the time. The permissive plugs and jacks have six pins. In the permissive arrangement, the phone company puts the ring lead directly on pin 3 and the tip lead on pin 4. The order code for this jack is RJ11C. The disadvantage of the permissive arrangement is that when local loop losses exceed -3 dBm, the transmit level cannot be increased. Also, when the modem is used on a private line where a 0 dBm level is feasible, one is forced to transmit at -9 dBm. However, since the permissive jack arrangement is identical to the jacks used in new telephone and extension telephone installations, the permissive arrangement allows a modem to be carried around and plugged in anywhere a telephone jack has been installed. In addition, a permissive modem plug can also plug into the other two types of jacks to be described.

The second registered connection arrangement is the fixed loss arrangement. In the fixed loss arrangement, the modem is set to transmit at -4 dBm. The phone company then provides whatever attenuation is required to achieve -12 dBm at the central office by adjusting a pad within the jack. The jack used in the fixed loss arrangement is the RJ41S and is called a universal jack. This jack and plug has eight wires, with the padded ring on pin 3 and the padded tip on pin 4. One disadvantage of this arrangement is that the receive signal, as well as the send signal, is attenuated. In addition, if a telephone set is attached to the modem, the ring and voice signals will also be attenuated.

In order to overcome these difficulties, the third arrangement the programmable, has been approved. In the programmable arrangement, the output level is controlled by a single resistor inside the jack. The value of the resistor is determined by the

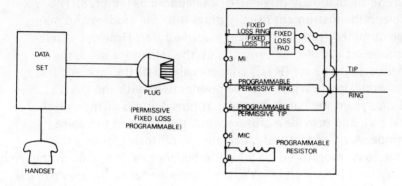

Figure 3-3/Circuit Diagram of the Universal Registered Jack Arrangement

phone company when the jack is installed. When the modem is plugged in, this resistor interacts with other resistors in the modem to set the transmit level at just the right point to achieve -12 dBm at the central office. Note that this resistor is not in series with the tip and ring leads, and therefore has no effect on the receive signal or on telephone set signals. The programmable jack has eight pins and its order code is RJ45S. The programming resistor pins are 7 and 8 and the tip and ring leads are 5 and 4.

If desired, the universal jack RJ41S used in the fixed loss arrangement may also be used in the programmable arrangement. The universal jack has a switch which allows it to operate with either plug. Figure 3-3 shows the universal jack circuitry. The permissive plug may also be used with the universal jack, because pins 3 and 4 of the 6-lead permissive plug connect to pins 4 and 5 of the 8-lead universal jack when the plug is inserted. In brief, any registered data set can connect to any universal jack, so one way to avoid confusion, although at extra cost, is to have only universal jacks installed (RJ41S).

39

If alternate voice communication is desired or if data calls are to be manually originated, a telephone is required. The telephone instrument usually plugs into the modem and may be obtained from the modem manufacturer. However, a telephone set can also be provided by the telephone company. This telephone set (RTC) connects ahead of the jack and has an exclusion key just like the phones used with the DAA's. Leads from the handset appear at pins 3 and 6 of the universal jack and provide a closure when the line is in the voice mode. A novel feature, called aural monitoring, allows the line to be monitored via a high-impedance bridge while in the data mode. As with DAA's, the telephone set or the modem may control the line. In the first case, all calls are originated, answered, or terminated manually. It is possible in this configuration to originate, answer, and terminate automatically if the handset is left off-hook and the exclusion key left in the lifted position. While possible, this procedure is not recommended, since a loose handset is easily damaged or accidentally replaced on-hook, and exclusion keys are prone to obey the law of gravity and move down. If the telephone set is optioned to permit the modem to control the line, then the modem always controls the line except when the handset is off-hook and the exclusion key is lifted. Going off-hook but leaving the exclusion key down permits aural monitoring. The state of the exclusion key appears as a contact closure between pins 3 and 6 of the universal jack.

4

The Joy of Frequency Shift Keying

Modems for Asynchronous Data

The voice network, either dial-up or leased line, is still the major conduit for digital data. To fit data which goes from dc to as high as 4800 Hz (ignoring harmonics) into a typical voice-line bandwidth of 300 to 3000 Hz requires special techniques. The most common method of accomplishing such bandwidth translation is modulation and demodulation, and the device that embodies the modulator and demodulator is the modem. Modems may be asynchronous or synchronous, two-wire or four-wire, half- or full-duplex, and dial network or leased line. In this chapter we describe the types of asynchronous modems commonly available and discuss how they work and how they can be used.

Frequency Shift Keying (FSK)

The simplest means of fitting data into the bandwidth of a voice line is to use the data to modulate a carrier. A carrier is simply a sine wave tone; to modulate it is to vary it in amplitude, frequency, or phase, as the data dictates. Phase modulation, as discussed in the next chapter, is practical only for synchronous data modems. Amplitude modulation is not used for asynchronous data transmission because of line noise problems and the fact that line losses vary so much that elaborate automatic gain control circuits would be necessary. Frequency modulation therefore is used almost universally. For binary data, one frequency of the carrier can represent a mark and one frequency can represent a space. This form of simple two-tone frequency modulation is called Frequency Shift Keying (FSK). The FSK waveform has no dc component and its spectral energy is concentrated in the middle of the voice band. The bandwidth actually used is about twice the data rate. FSK is the modulation technique used in the 202- and 103-type modems discussed below.

43

Basic 202 Modem

The simplest of the FSK modems is the 202. The number refers to the Bell system unit and is used universally to describe FSK modems with the characteristics described in this section. The 202 transmits a tone of 1200 Hz when marking and one of 2200 Hz when spacing; it can handle data rates from 0 to 1200 baud (to 1800 baud on good lines). The 202 is available in many different configurations for use on two-point or multipoint private lines or switched networks. For switched network use the data rate usually is specified as limited to 1200 baud, but it should be understood that the modem does not have to be strapped or informed in any way of the data rate. It is possible to switch a terminal from, say, 600 to 1200 baud without doing anything to the modem. It is also possible to operate on the dial network at 1800 baud if a good connection is made, despite the limitation on paper to 1200 baud. C2 line conditioning usually is recommended for best results at 1800 baud on private lines.

At the heart of the transmitter of the 202 is usually a digital counter driven by a crystal oscillator, the divisor of which depends directly on the state of the data. When the frequency of the carrier is shifted, care must be taken so that no abrupt phase change occurs — such a change would cause perturbations on the line and errors at the remote receiver. This type of FSK modulation is called phase continuous or phase coherent. When such a line is monitored, a pure tone is heard only if the data is continually marking or spacing. With actual data, the sound on the line is like white noise or a rushing atonal static.

After filtering, amplification, and limiting, an FSK demodulator in the receiver recovers the original data. Most demodulators used today are digital. In the digital counting method, the time between consecutive zero crossings of the carrier is measured by counting a high frequency reference squarewave. A high count indicates that the carrier is at 1200 Hz and therefore marking. A low count indicates a carrier of 2200 Hz and therefore spacing.

44

Leased Line 202's

202's can be used on either four-wire or two-wire private lines. In four-wire service, the modem can be operated full-duplex so that data can be sent and received simultaneously. In this case, the modems keep carrier on continuously in both directions. In this instance, the only EIA control signal which has any real meaning is Carrier Detect, which should be on continuously at both ends.

With a 202 on a two-wire private line, the operation is more complex. First, a circuit called a hybrid is added to the modem. A hybrid allows both the 202 transmitter and receiver to connect to the same pair of wires and terminates the line in the proper impedance (usually 600 Ω). The hybrid is essentially a four-wire-to-two-wire converter, but it has other functions, as discussed below regarding the 103-type modems. Only half-duplex operation is possible with a 202 on a two-wire line. Thus it is necessary to use RTS and CTS signals to tell the modem when to transmit and when to receive.

In a two-wire system, if carrier is turned off abruptly when RTS is lowered, the remote receiver is subjected to a line turnoff transient and any ensuing line noise. It is therefore desirable to tell the remote modem receiver that carrier is about to turn off so that it can inhibit its receive data function. This turnoff is activated by shifting the carrier to 900 Hz for a period of 10 ms or 30 ms before it is turned off completely. This feature of the 202 is called soft carrier turnoff.

The turning off of Request to Send indicates a desire to receive, but reception cannot begin immediately. The hard or soft carrier signals still may be reverberating on the line, and the remote carrier may not have arrived yet and only noise therefore would be demodulated. Thus the receiver must be disabled during the time between termination of Request to Send and the start of Carrier Detect. The process of disabling the receiver after Request to Send is lowered is called squelching, and squelch periods of 50 ms or 150 ms are typical. The squelch time required depends on the round-trip propagation delay of the line involved. The function of keeping the demodulator inactive in the absence of carrier is called clamping. In a typical 202, the carrier-detect circuit can detect the presence of carrier in about 40 ms. Thus, a terminal that has been receiving cannot begin to transmit until the soft carrier-turnoff time, the squelch time, and the carrier-acquisition time have elapsed. This period determines the Request to Send/Clear to Send delay; for the 202 on a two-wire long-distance line, it is about 200 ms.

Use of the 202 on the Dial Network

202's used on the dial network are very similar to those used on two-wire private lines. The principal additional functions required are autoanswer, autodisconnect, and echo-suppressor management. The additional active EIA control signals required include Data Terminal Ready, Ring Indicator, and Data Set Ready. A dial network 202 which connects directly to the phone line looks for a 20 to 30 Hz, 55 to 110 V, pulsed ringing signal. If Data Terminal Ready is present when ringing is detected, the modem will answer the call by placing a load on the line that can sink 20 to 120 mA and is less than 200 Ω at dc. The modem raises Data Set Ready and, after a period of about 1.5 s (to allow the telephone central office to react to the off-hook state of the modem), outputs 2 to 5 s of 2025 Hz. This answer tone, as it is called, serves to tell the originating station that it has reached an active data set. The tone also serves to disable any echo suppressors that may be present on lines longer than 1000 mi. After the answer-tone period, the tone either reverts to 1200 Hz if the input is marking, or disappears entirely if Request to Send is off. If there is no tone on the line in either direction for 50 ms, the echo suppressor will be re-enabled. This is of little significance if the RTS-CTS delay is set at 200 ms since the echo suppressors will have time to turn around during the squelch and clamp period. The originating 202 raises Data Set Ready and holds the line as soon as the data button is depressed by the operator when answer tone is heard.

Automatic disconnection usually is initiated by lowering Data Terminal Ready. If one end disconnects in this manner, the other end should hang up as well — if it can detect the reversal or momentary loss of dc line current when the central office terminates a call. Abort timers are quite useful in aborting calls after wrong numbers or if line current disconnect is not possible. The abort timer is set to initiate a disconnect if neither Request to Send nor carrier is present for a set period, typicall 15 s to 1 min. It is surprising, however, how many systems are dormant for longer than 1 min, thereby leading to false disconnects if the abort-timer option is used.

202's with Reverse Channel

Since the FSK spectrum of the 202 does not include much energy in the low-frequency region between 300 and 400 Hz, it is possible to put a second carrier in this region. Typically this channel is used to send a 387 Hz tone. The tone may be turned on and off up to five times a second. The reverse channel can serve many functions that have little to do with the transmission of actual data. One such function is simply to keep the echo suppressor disabled. The reverse channel tone ordinarily is transmitted whenever main channel Request to Send is off. Thus some tone is always present on the line — just what is needed to keep the echo suppressor off the line once it has been disabled by the answer tone. A second communications function of the reverse channel is to improve the abort timer disconnect function so that disconnect occurs only if Request to Send and both main channel and reverse channel carriers are off. Data-oriented functions of this slow-speed reverse channel include request for retransmission of a previous data block (ARQ) and interruption of a transmission (break).

Some non-Bell 202 modems have been manufactured with secondary channels that can handle data up to 150 baud. These secondary channels are of the FSK type with mark and space frequencies of 375 and 475 Hz, respectively. The secondary channel is often independent of the main channel and has its own Request to Send, Clear to Send, and Carrier Detect functions. If such a channel is used independently of the main channel, it cannot be relied upon to keep echo suppressors disabled.

1200 baud Acoustic Couplers

It is possible to couple a 202 modem to the dial network acoustically. Because of the distortions in most handsets, 1200 baud is the maximum data rate recommended. Usually an acoustic coupler at one end talks to a hard-wired 202 at the other end. Acoustically-coupled 202's also feature the reverse-channel and most other standard 202 options. If two acoustically-coupled 202 modems are connected, one of them must have a manually-activated answer-tone generator switch in order to deactivate the echo suppressor. The local-copy-option switch (sometimes mislabeled "full-duplex") loops data in the coupler or hard-wired modem so that the terminal receives what it transmits.

Multidrop Systems Using 202's

In a multidrop system, a four-wire line interconnects a master modem with many remote modems bridged on the line. The master modem transmits carrier continuously to all of the remote stations; thus there is no RTS-CTS delay needed when data is transmitted by this central modem. As the remote stations are polled, they in turn bring up carrier, and the central modem must acquire this carrier. Normally it takes 20 ms on a private line to acquire carrier, but a fast carrier-acquisition option has been developed — it reduces this time to as little as 6 ms if a pulse is applied to pin 25 of the EIA interface each time a terminal is polled in order to reset the Carrier Detect circuitry and prime it for fast acquisition.

48

103-Type Modems

A major disadvantage of the 202 modem is that it is half-duplex and can be used only with terminals and computers that are intelligent enough to use the Request to Send/Clear to Send leads in the EIA interface. The 103 series modems (103, 101, 108, and 113) are full-duplex on two-wire lines and therefore are simpler for the computer to control (even though computers rarely send and receive data at the same time). The 103 is analogous to a 202 modem equipped with a secondary channel, except that the bandwidth of the line is shared equally so that both channels can operate at the same data rate. The 103 type of modem also can be described as a two-channel frequency division multiplexer — one FSK channel operates using 2225 Hz for marks and 2025 Hz for spaces, the other uses 1270 Hz for marks and 1070 for spaces. With a frequency shift of 200 Hz it is possible to reliably handle data rates of up to 300 baud. There are of necessity two basic kinds of 103's which must be used together in all applications. The originate type of 103 transmits on the lower band centered around 2125 Hz. Thus, the 103-type modem contains a transmitter and receiver that normally cannot talk to one another. The names "answer" and "originate" are arbitrary and have meaning only in dial network applications, in which the originate type is used by the persion dialing the call and the answer type is placed at the computer site where the incoming call is answered. However, when private-line use or manual dialing and manual answering are involved, the names need have no meaning as long as one of each type is used.

Leased Line 103's

A pair of 103's (103F or 108) can be used on a two-wire leased line to provide 300 baud FDX data communications. No EIA control signals except Carrier Detect need be used in this straight-forward application. (The same modems also can be used via CDT data access arrangements in low-cost manual

49

originate and answer systems on short dial network connections. On longer calls, it is necessary to disable the echo suppressors, which can be done manually by marking the answer modem for half a second before the originate modem is put on the line.) 103's can be used as well in multidrop configurations which employ lower-cost two-wire lines. Four-wire lines also can be used; they must be used if the 103 is not equipped with a hybrid. In the 103, the hybrid network keeps transmit carrier from reaching the receiver input and possibly overloading it or overwhelming a low-level received carrier signal. Of course, as in any multidrop system, the remote 103 modems must operate in the controlled carrier mode with Request to Send/Clear to Send protocol. Older modems required a Clear to Send delay of some 265 ms but newer models can operate with only an 8.5 ms delay, thereby making 103 polling networks more efficient.

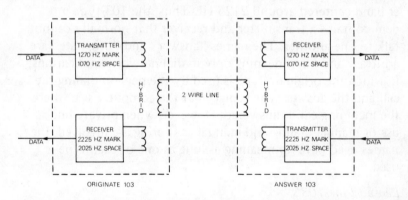

Figure 4-1/An Originate 103 Must Talk to an Answer 103.

103's in Dial Network Applications

The originate 103 (113A) modem is similar to the private-line modem except for the addition of a telephone handset and line-holding and disconnect circuits. A data call is dialed in the normal manner and, when the data/talk button is pressed, the modem takes control of the line. Disconnection can be manual or automatic (discussed below). Originate modems also include provisions for working with the automatic calling units described in Chapter 6.

When someone originates a data call to a computer, it is far more convenient for all concerned for that call to be answered automatically by the computer. To accomplish this, an auto-answer 103 is required. Remember that, although not all answer-type 103's can autoanswer, all autoanswer 103's are of the answer type. The autoanswer type of 103 (113B), like the 202, detects ring and, if DTR is on, goes off-hook, raises Data Set Ready, and, after the silent period, puts 2225 Hz on the line to disable the echo suppressors and tell the originator that a data set has been reached. The 2225 Hz remains on the line until the answering modem detects carrier from the originating end. In dial network 103 modems, Request to Send is not used, but Clear to Send may be. Clear to Send in this case means that the answer tone and carrier acquisition processes at the beginning of a call have been completed. CTS and Carrier Detect usually come on and stay on for the duration of a call. Indeed, in many 103 modems, the two signals are tied together; in such cases, computers should not transmit until they are receiving carrier. Depending on the vintage of the originate modem, Data Set Ready may come on either when the modem is put in the data mode or when carrier is received from the answering end. There is a third type of 103 which is somewhat intelligent, the autoanswer/originate 103. In an autoanswer/originate 103, the detection of ring signal causes the modem to switch to the answer set of send and receive frequencies; otherwise, the modem remains in the originate state.

51

Automatic Disconnection of Calls by 103 Modems

103's have many ways to end a call. As in the 202, the 103 modem can be commanded by the computer to drop the line by lowering Data Terminal Ready, or the modems at either end can be optioned to hang up calls if carrier is lost for over 100 ms. Thus the computer can execute both remote and local disconnects by dropping DTR, causing the local modem to hang up, and inducing a loss-of-carrier disconnect at the remote end. Note that in some 103 modems carrier can be reacquired only after a brief line hit if the mark frequency is present. Such modems are likely to suffer from unexpected disconnects if the loss-of-carrier disconnect option is used. A reliable method that can be used with or without the loss-of-carrier disconnect is called long-space disconnect. In this method, when DTR is lowered (or a long loss of carrier is detected), the modem transmits 3s of the spacing frequency before it hangs up. The modem at the other end, upon receiving either 400 ms or 1.5 s of spacing, likewise disconnects. If a computer is not equipped to lower Data Terminal Ready to initiate this process, it can output the spaces as a break signal on the data leads, causing the remote modem to hang up, which in turn causes the local modems to hang up due to loss of carrier.

If the above methods still do not suffice (perhaps because the terminal or computer can neither lower DTR nor send continuous spaces, or because the modem lacks these options), one can hang up manually at one end and cause a disconnect at the other, via the dc line holding current circuit discussed for the 202. Like the 202, the 103 can be equipped with an abort timer which causes a disconnect at the beginning of a call if carrier has not been acquired in 20 to 30 s. The abort timer period starts when ring is detected in the answering modem or, if originating, when the modem is put into the data mode. In the answer/originate modem it is possible to have the abort timer function in autoanswer but not in manual originate.

52

103 Acoustic Couplers

103 modems can connect to the phone line acoustically. Usually an acoustically-coupled modem calls an autoanswer hard-wired unit at the other end. Thus, most acoustic couplers are of the originate type. It is possible to get answer or answer/originate couplers, but on long calls the echo-suppressing function of the autoanswering modem must be duplicated manually by the operator of the answer-type acoustic coupler. Since all 103's are full-duplex devices, the HDX-FDX switches found on many couplers do not refer to communications protocol, but rather to a local-copy option which permits a terminal to look at what it is sending (if it does not already have this capability). Most originate acoustic couplers cannot transmit carrier unless they are receiving carrier.

Full-Duplex 1200 Baud Modems

Several full-duplex modems analogous to the 103 have been developed that permit 600 or 1200 baud asynchronous data to be sent and received simultaneously on a two-wire line. These modems are not FSK modems. They use synchronous modulation techniques (discussed in the next chapter) and must convert the asynchronous data to synchronous form before it can be transmitted. Sometimes these full-duplex, high-speed modems are sensitive to code structure and data rate. One of the first of these modems strips off the rest bits before transmitting the data, and thus can work only with start-stop data that has a ten-bit or other specific structure. Other, later designs actually can transmit 1200 bps of synchronous random data; therefore, when they transmit asynchronous data, they simply synchronize themselves to the data and become format transparent. Such a format-transparent modem can transmit encrypted data, facsimile data, and the 511- or 2047-bit patterns used in much communications test equipment. An interesting feature of a self-synchronizing modem is that it can operate equally well at integer

53

submultiples of the 1200 baud rate (such as 600 baud or 300 baud) without strapping. At rates lower than 300 baud, so many samples of the data are being sent that the data rate can be anything. Thus this modem behaves like a 103 at rates below 300 baud, but requires its data to be within 1% of the nominal rate at the higher speeds such as 600 or 1200 baud. Data buffers take care of any odd-length stop bits.

The Bell version of the full-duplex 202 (212A) goes one step further — it uses two 475 Hz bands centered around carriers of 1200 Hz and 2400 Hz when handling 1200 baud data, but switches to the 103 carrier frequencies when it answers a call from a 103 data set. Unfortunately, none of these modems has proved reliable when used with acoustic couplers. Therefore, the fastest reliable FDX data rate via acoustic couplers is still 300 baud, with some non-standard units running at 450 or 600 baud.

5

Trans-cendental Modulation

Modems for Synchronous Data

The simplest form of synchronous modem is the synchronous 202. Any standard 202 modem can be used synchronously by adding both a clock generator to the transmitter in order to clock the data source, and a simple clock-recovery circuit at the other end to extract clock from the received data. This is achieved by allowing data transitions to correct and phase an essentially free-running clock. Provided there are enough data transitions to keep this clock in step, there is little chance of error; a simple data scrambler can be added to insure plenty of data transitions. Ultimately, though, we would still have a modem limited to 1800 bps. Thus, it is not synchronization *per se* that makes possible higher data rates, but rather the multilevel coding and modulation techniques that synchronous operation permits.

In the 103 and 202 modems considered so far, the data and signaling rates have been identical (with start and stop bits considered as data bits), and the bits have equalled the bauds. But suppose we allow each baud to represent more than one bit. We have not altered the signaling rate and therefore are not exceeding the limits of information theory. But if bauds are to represent more than one bit apiece, they each must be capable of assuming more than just two levels (as in FSK); if such signaling elements are going to be multilevel, it is also necessary to know exactly when to measure their values. For were we to look at the signal at just any time, we might observe it as it is passing through an intermediate level and thereby make a wrong decision. This situation illustrates the need for synchronization — a clock is needed to indicate precisely when the line signal should be sampled in order to determine its true value.

Multilevel signaling elements are more susceptible to misinterpretation due to noise and other line perturbations than are binary signaling elements. Thus, advanced signal processing procedures and special multilevel modulation techniques are required to improve performance. In the following sections we describe the many ways in which coding and multilevel modulation have been put into practice to make reliable modems that operate at 2400, 4800, 7200, and 9600 bps.

Basic 201 Modem

The simplest of the synchronous modems is the 201, which operates at 2000 or 2400 bps. In the 201 the bits are taken two at a time to form dibits; there are only four possible dibits (00, 01, 10, and 11). The 201 uses a modulation technique called Differential Phase Shift Keying (DPSK), and each dibit causes a shift in phase by a specific amount. Since there are four dibits, there are four possible phase shifts. Each dibit is assigned a value of phase shift such that, if the receiver makes the most likely error of picking an adjacent signal phase, only a one-bit error will be produced. In particular, the 201 shifts phase 45° for the dibit 00, 135° for the dibit 10, 225° for 11, and 315° for 01. Note that contiguous phase angles or adjacent quadrants differ by only one bit. The phase shift here is differential, meaning that each of the above phase shifts is referenced to the phase of the carrier during the previous dibit interval.

The advantages of this method are that no zero phase reference tone need be transmitted or synthesized, and an abrupt phase step on the line causes only a single dibit error. Note also that there is a phase change of at least 45° every dibit interval, a fact which is important to the receiver, as described below. Finally, these phase changes are made to a carrier of 1800 Hz if the modem is operating at 2400 bps, and to 1750 Hz if the data rate is 2000 bps. The respective equivalent signaling rates are 1200 and 1000 baud, which are well below the maximum signaling rate of the 202 modem (1800 baud); indeed, the spectrum of the 201 modem is contained easily within the limits of 600 to 3000 Hz, leaving plenty of room for a reverse or secondary channel. The 201 receiver provides fixed compromise amplitude and delay distortion equalizers, which are switched in or out to minimize the error rate on a given line.

Most 201 receivers use a method called coherent detection to recover the dibits. A local or reference voltage-controlled oscillator is kept running at the carrier frequency. Each time a dibit is received, this oscillator is set to the nominal phase of the dibit assumed to have been transmitted. When the next set of carrier cycles arrives, its phase is compared with the phase of the reference carrier, and a decision is made as to what phase change has occurred and, therefore, what pair of bits has been sent. The reference carrier phase then is updated and the process is repeated for the next dibit. The difference between the phase shifts that actually are observed and the nominal values of 45, 135, 225, and 315° provides a measure of the line quality; many modems display this signal besides outputting it, or use it to control the carrier detect lead.

By mathematical permutations it is possible to demonstrate that the four-phase signal generated by the 201 modem actually consists of two 1800 Hz carriers 90° apart in phase, each amplitude-modulated by a dc to 600 Hz signal representing each half of the dibit. This concept leads to a different implementation of the coherent detection scheme, whereby the received carrier is amplitude demodulated twice — using an in-phase reference carrier, and once using a 90° phase reference carrier. The resulting baseband signals can then be processed separately to recover the dibit halves they represent.

A straightforward, largely digital demodulator can be implemented by translating the received and reference carriers to higher frequencies, then counting the time between zero crossings of the carrier cycles that lie at the center of the dibit interval.

All these methods of detection depend on being able to recover a stable dibit clock (1200 or 1000 bps) from the received carrier so that the phase change decisions can be made with the proper periodicity and at the correct moment. Fortunately, when the phase of the carrier changes every dibit period (as in this case), the spectrum of the carrier signal always contains some energy at 1200 or 1000 Hz. This dibit clock energy can be extracted by means of a sharply tuned filter, and used to control the frequency of a dibit clock generator. The phase of this dibit clock also must be adjusted so that the carrier phase is read at the center of the dibit interval. The center of the dibit interval can be found by using the line quality error signals referred to earlier. For instance, if the error between the observed and theoretical phase differences is the same over many consecutive dibits, the moment of sampling must be too early or too late. The dibit clock then is retarded or advanced appropriately in order to minimize the average phase error signal.

In theory, there is absolutely no reason why each bit of the dibit must originate from the same data source. The 201 could handle two 1200 bps sources just as easily as one 2400 bps source. Though no such split-stream 2400 bps modem to our knowledge has been put on the market, this principle is quite important in the higher-speed world. Some 201's are equipped with a switch to shift the data speed to 1200 bps, by bringing the dibit clock to pins 15 and 17 at the EIA interface. In this instance, all dibits are either 00 or 11.

Full duplex 1200 bps modems may be constructed by combining two four-phase modems, each operating at a different send and receive carrier frequency. In each channel the dibit signaling rate is only 600 baud; therefore both channels can operate simultaneously within the 3000 Hz typically available on a voice line.

Another novelty in the 201 field is the speed adaptive 201. This is a 201 modem that switches itself between 2000 and 2400 bps on the basis of the received carrier frequency. Such a modem is particularly useful in timesharing systems where

60

auto-answering modems receive calls from many remote users.

System Applications of 201 Modems

The 201 modem can be used on four-wire lines in the full-duplex mode, and on multidrop two-wire private or dial-up lines in the half-duplex mode. The 201 modem is a good choice for multidrop applications because of its relatively short Request to Send/Clear to Send time of about 8 ms. When used on two-wire lines, however, this modem's turn-around time must be lengthened to about 150 ms, to allow for squelch and clamp periods, as described for the 202. Early 201's had rather slow-acting clock recovery circuits; thus, the response time in multidrop applications could not be minimized. Therefore, a feature called new sync was introduced. New sync reduces polling delays by resetting carrier detect and in some cases by erasing the memory of the previous receive clock thus allowing immediate acquisition of both carrier and the next receive clock. To accomplish this end, the computer is required to pulse the modem each time it polls a new remote terminal, using either pin 14 or 11 in the EIA interface. This option, is used very rarely nowadays, since few computers support it and new modem designs can lock onto a new receive data clock as fast as carrier can be acquired.

The Basic 208 Modem (4800 bps)

Unlike the phone company's 201, which virtually all other manufacturers except IBM adopted as a standard, the model 208 (4800 bps) modem, offered by the Bell system, is just one of many. Thus, unless a manufacturer clearly states that his modem is compatible with the 208, it probably isn't. Nevertheless, we will concentrate here on the 208 because it is typical of the state of the art in 4800 bps transmission.

The 208 is quite similar to the 201 in principle. It is also a DPSK modem, but it uses eight phase instead of four phase

61

differential phase shift on a carrier of 1800 Hz. The data bits are taken three at a time to form tribits. After Grey encoding, each of the eight possible tribits is assigned an angle starting at 22.5° for the tribit 000 and 67.5° for 001, and going in 45° increments up to 337.5° (-22.5°) for 100. The assignment of a specific tribit to an angle is done in such a manner (Grey encoding) that the most likely error in demodulation (45°) will cause only a 1-bit error.

Since the bits are taken three at a time, the signalling rate is 1600 baud. One could easily take data from three different sources of 1600 bps data but it would be difficult to handle 2400 bps channels. That is the reason why there are so few split-stream 4800 bps modems on the market. One can assemble tribits by alternately taking two bits from one channel and one from the other, but this requires a synchronization circuit to make sure the recovered tribits are sorted out properly. In general, therefore, dual stream DPSK modems are rare.

In order to demodulate the eight-phase signal as described below, it is necessary to ensure that a 1600 baud tribit clock can be recovered reliably from the received waveform. There will only be enough such 1600 baud energy if the phase of the carrier changes randomly at this rate. That this is so can be seen by imagining a continuous 001 data stream applied to the modulator. After Grey encoding, each tribit remains 001, and therefore the phase of the carrier is delayed by 67.5°, tribit after tribit. Constantly shifting a carrier in this manner is essentially the same as shifting it in frequency. Shifting an 1800 Hz carrier 67.5° every 1/1600th of a second and passing it through a 3000 Hz bandpass circuit such as a phone line just produces a 1500 Hz carrier with almost no energy at 1600 Hz. If, however, the carrier is shifted randomly at each tribit time, a wideband signal is produced with energy at many frequencies including 1600 Hz. Another way to understand this principle is to consider that a DPSK signal is actually a double sideband signal whose frequency components

62

are separated by the data modulation rate. If the data has enough transitions to look like a 1600 bps data signal, then the first frequency components of the upper and lower sidebands will be separated from the carrier by 800 Hz, and this timing energy can be recovered. To insure that the tribits change randomly enough to have a strong 1600 bps component, a data scrambler is used. The scrambler ensures that the modem is transparent to virtually any realistic data pattern.

Scramblers are logic circuits that add data to the pseudo-random output of a small shift register. The demodulator must subtract an identical pseudo-random pattern to recover the data. Obviously the scrambler and descramblers must be exactly synchronized or the data cannot be recovered. Scramblers may be either self-synchronizing or synchronized by sending synchronization patterns. Since it is inconvenient to interrupt the flow of data to send synchronization patterns and because it is difficult to detect loss of synchronization, most modems use self-synchronizing scramblers. The major disadvantage of a self-synchronizing scrambler is that the received scrambled data stream passes through the pseudo-random generator in the descrambling process (see Chapter 10), and any error in transmission will be multiplied. In the 208 such a self-scrambling method is used, but the error multiplication effect has been considerably minimized.

In a typical 208, every third bit of data is randomized by a succession of three seven-bit shift registers with feedback from the fourth and seventh stages in each register. This first bit of the tribit is then scrambled again in a fourth seven-bit register which is specially designed to eliminate patterns that repeat every eight tribits. The middle bit of the tribit is randomized by mixing it with a delayed replica of the scrambled first bit. The third bit is likewise randomized by being mixed with the scrambled middle bit and a delayed replica of the scrambled first bit. These bits therefore do not pass through the scrambler and have no effect on its pattern. The first bit of the scrambled tribit represents changes of 180°, the middle 90°, and the third 45°. When all three bits are randomized, all eight possible phase angles become equally probable, which provides enough energy for the demodulator to extract baud timing. Since only the first bit is used to generate the self-synchronizing pseudo-random stream and since this bit is represented by a 180° phase shift, the more likely demodulation errors of 45° or 90° will not affect the synchronization of the descrambler. Therefore it is possible to have self-synchronization without substantial error multiplication. It is true, however, that an error in the first bit will be likely to cause an error in the other two, and an error in the middle bit will cause an error in the third.

The tribit output of the scrambler is handled digitally to generate a digital replica of the phase-shifted 1800 Hz carrier. A digital-to-analog converter, low-pass filter, and compromise equalization network complete the basic transmitter.

The 208 Receiver

After passing through an automatic gain-control amplifier and band-pass filter to remove out-of-band noise, the carrier signal passes through an adaptive equalizer (described below) to the demodulator. In the demodulator, the carrier is frequency translated, so that there will be nine carrier cycles per signalling element. A high-frequency clock is then used to measure the time between the recovered midband 1600-baud clock edge and the first positive edge of the carrier cycle in progress. Successive values of this count can then be compared digitally to determine the phase shift during the previous signalling interval. The phase shift as measured is the sum of the nominal phase shift of the modulator, plus error signals due to line noise, and errors in the demodulator, such as a timing error in the 1600 baud clock. The measured phase difference is rounded off to the nearest nominal value, and the equivalent tribit is then unscrambled and Grey decoded to recover the data. The difference between the nominal and measured values of phase is an error signal which, if consistently very large, is used to force the adaptive equalizer to go through a complete re-equalization cycle (see below). This error signal is also used to light an error lamp on the front panel and turn off the signal quality lead on the EIA connector. The error threshold at which the modem alarms in this manner is about one error in a thousand bits.

The frequency-translated carrier is also full-wave rectified, and filtered to recover the 1600 Hz energy needed to stabilize the 1600 baud clock recovery circuit.

Adaptive Equalization

The purpose of any equalizer is to compensate for fixed, or very slowly varying, line distortions. The major such distortion is delay distortion, where the transmission delay through the line varies with frequency. Since this line delay distortion does not vary rapidly, it is possible to eliminate its major effects by the use of networks known as delay equalizers. Early 4800 bps modems contained equalizers that were adjusted manually for the lowest error signal. But, not only was the adjustment procedure tedious, it also was not feasible for use in multipoint or dial-network applications where frequent re-equalization is necessary, or even on private lines, where parameters often drift with time of day or temperature. The 208 was therefore equipped with a self-adjusting equalizer which, after a short initial training period, continues to adjust itself to minimize the average phase error.

One way to understand the inner workings of an adaptive equalizer is to realize that because of phone-line delay distortion, each pulse of carrier arrives at the receiver preceded by the faster-travelling elements of itself and trailed by its slower components. Thus the line signal observed at any moment is a composite of the present signal element and contributions from other elements just ahead and just behind it. The adaptive equalizer is designed to cancel this intersymbol interference.

65

The adaptive equalizer in the 208 consists of two parts: a tapped six-stage delay line and a correction calculator. Each segment of the delay line is equal to the signalling interval (625 msec). The basic equalization technique consists of cancelling any intersymbol disturbances in the central signal element by adding or subtracting voltages derived from the other six delay line taps, representing three carrier signal elements ahead of and behind the element then being demodulated. The correction calculator decides what polarity and what amplitude is needed from each tap to minimize the intersymbol interference. In the 208, voltage from each tap is fed to two variable gain amplifiers. Two amplifiers are used for each tap so that corrections can be made independently both in-phase and in quadrature phase. This technique improves the accuracy of the equalization process but does not require a second delay line or extra taps. The outputs from the six in-phase gain controls are summed together and then combined with the center signal to cancel the in-phase interference. The outputs of the quadrature phase gain controls are likewise added together, phase shifted 90°, and then combined with the center signal to cancel the quadrature phase interference. The cleaned-up center tap carrier signal can then be demodulated with little error due to delay distortion.

The question still remains as to how the twelve gain controls can be set to minimize the average demodulation error. The correction calculator does this using the phase error signal developed in the demodulator. At each cycle of the baud clock, the calculator is given the nominal phase of the carrier determined by the demodulator. Thus the calculator at any given moment has in storage the value of these signals for the last seven cycles. The first and last three values of phase angle are converted to sine and cosine values to use in calculating the in-phase and quadrature-phase gain settings. At each cycle of the 1600 baud clock, the phase error of the middle element of the calculator is multiplied by the twelve sines and cosines. The twelve products developed in this way are then individually integrated to produce a dc voltage that controls the polarity and amplitude of the variable gain controls described above. The values of phase and phase error used to calculate the gain settings have nothing to do with the data being demodulated at that instant. Actually, the settings of the equalizer are updated three elements later, and due to the time constant of the integrator, the equalizer is even further behind the demodulator.

It is not intuitively obvious that the integrated product of the nominal element phase angle and the phase error is a voltage proportional to the intersymbol interference contribution of the element. After all, the phase error signal includes errors from all the preceding and following elements. How can we decide how to vary the gain of just one elemental signal to cancel its contribution to the total error? Well, first let us assume that the element under consideration does not cause any intersymbol interference. Since the tribits have been scrambled, the values of phase angle (and therefore the sines and cosines) will assume positive and negative values that over a period of time will average zero. The sines and cosines are multiplied by a phase error signal which may be constant or random. In both cases, the integrated product and the gain will be zero, since the randomness of the phase error is independent of the randomness of the element phase. Now let us assume that the element we are observing does cause intersymbol interference because its cancellation gain circuit is not adjusted properly. We would then see that each time the sine is large, the phase error would be large. Furthermore, positive sine values would produce different size errors than negative sine values. Thus, after integration there would be a net dc value, and this would cause a readjustment of the gain in the direction to reduce the phase error.

System Considerations When Adaptive Equalizers Are Used

Because of the integrators and other delays, it takes a fair amount of time for an adaptive equalizer to adjust itself on random data. The adjustment process can be accelerated substantially if a training pattern can be sent before data each time carrier is turned on. The training pattern in the 208 consists of twelve tribits chosen so that only four phases, rather than eight, are used. This makes it easier for the demodulator to find the nominal phase while the equalizer is still untrained. This is followed by a four-phase, 17-tribit pattern repeated three times, during which the equalizer adjusts itself, and finally, an eight-phase series of 13 all-mark scrambled tribits to synchronize the receive scrambler. All this takes about 50 milliseconds; therefore the clear-to-send delay of the 208 is 50 milliseconds minimum. On long-distance circuits, a clear-to-send delay of 150 msec may be needed to counteract the effects of transients and echoes on long lines.

Because of the 50 msec training time, which is the equivalent of 240 bits, it may not be of advantage to run at 4800 bps in multidrop networks, or even in dial-up systems if the average block size is smaller than 250 bits or 32 bytes. In such cases, the 201 is probably the more economical choice.

When the phase error is excessive for a period of time, the 208 will automatically enter a retraining mode during which it outputs only marks to the terminal until the phase error has been again minimized. This auto retrain feature can be strapped off, but if used, the computer and terminal should be able to cope with the interruption in data when it does occur.

Dial Network Applications of the 208

The 208A may be used on 4-wire private lines and the 208B on the dial network using two wires. When a 208B is called, it automatically answers the call, and after a short quiet period it outputs a 2025 Hz answer tone for two seconds to disable the echo suppressor. If Request to Send is not on, and carrier is not being received, the 208B puts 600 Hz on the line to hold the echo suppressors off. In general it is better if only

68

one 208 is strapped to put 600 Hz on such an idle line in order to lessen the chance that 600 Hz distortion will activate the carrier detect circuit.

The 208B also incorporates automatic test features that enable any 208 dial-up modem to be tested from a central test site. A test message is sent to the modem, which checks it for errors and returns a test message report to the test center. This cycle repeats every one or two seconds for as long as desired.

New Developments in 4800 bps Modems

By using more sophisticated adaptive equalizer circuit techniques it is possible to speed up the convergence time of the equalizer and thereby increase the throughput in half-duplex situations. One simple technique is to start transmission at 2400 bps and then shift to 4800 bps as soon as the equalizer is ready. This method reduces the Clear to Send time to an equivalent value of about 23 msec, even though transmission begins at 2400 bps after 9 msec. Microprocessor designs or fast, all-digital equalization calculators can achieve RTS-CTS delays as small as 14 msec, or reduce it still further by storing the equalizer parameters and recalling them after each turnaround. The Bell 208 does not make provision for remote loopback tests, reverse channel, or automatic dial back-up. These features are, however, available from non-Bell makers of 4800 bps modems.

9600 bps Modems

The techniques that enable 9600 bps to be transmitted over private voice-grade lines are truly transcendental, and in some designs, herculean. In general, 9600 bps is limited to point-to-point FDX 4-wire leased-line or two-phone-call dial-up applications, becasue the retraining and turnaround times have been too long for efficient use in most polling or 2-wire dial-up configurations. Although many 9600 bps modems require conditioned lines, some units, particularly those using vestigial sideband modulation, can often operate on unconditioned lines, including most dial-up lines; they therefore can incorporate dial backup options. All 9600 bps modems can also operate at 7200 or 4800 bps in the dial backup mode if necessary. Of course, new techniques, such as the equalizer coefficient memory discussed above for 4800 bps modems, will make half-duplex operation at 9600 bps more practical.

While it would be possible to take the bits four at a time and assign them to sixteen carrier phases, the phase difference between adjacent symbols would be 22.5°, and phase jitter on a line of only 11.25° would cause an error. Since phase jitter is a major source of error, even at 4800 bps (where the jitter must reach 22.5° to cause an error) it is obvious that the sixteen-phase DPSK technique is not good enough for a practical long-haul 9600 bps modem.

There are two modulation techniques which can be shown to be more effective than DPSK where high data rates are concerned. The first of these techniques is vestigial sideband modulation, or VSB; the second is quadrature amplitude modulation, or QAM. Despite much discussion and analysis over the years, no one has been able to demonstrate the theoretical superiority of one technique over another when all the different types of line impairments are present together. One thing is clear, however — the latest VSB modems do not require line conditioning, whereas most QAM modems suggest that C2 conditioning will substantially reduce the error rate. A second difference is in the complexity of the modems. The VSB modems, as will be seen below, are much less complex and therefore cost from 30% to 50% less than QAM modems. The high performance of both QAM and VSB modems at 9600 bps is made possible by the use of extremely sophisticated adaptive equalizers. Whereas the 208 modem needed only a six-element delay line, the QAM modems typically incorporate 30-stage adaptive equalizers, and the latest VSB modems use 60 stages. It is clear that the manner in which the modulation technique is implemented and sup-

70

ported by equalizers, automatic gain-control circuits, carrier and timing recovery circuits, and scramblers is probably more important than the modulation technique used. As we shall see, even among QAM advocates there is no unanimity as to which type of QAM is best. In the balance of this chapter we shall describe a variety of modulation techniques in the hope that the reader will then be able to choose the modem that best meets his special needs.

VSB 9600 bps Modems

We have seen that the double sideband signal of the 202 modem can transmit data at a rate of 1800 bps. Therefore single or vestigial sideband FM could transmit 3600 baud, since the entire bandwidth could be used for the one sideband. Unfortunately, vestigial sideband FM is not possible, because it cannot be demodulated. But vestigial sideband AM is possible; when synchronous modulation and demodulation techniques are used in conjunction with VSB, it is possible to signal at 4800 baud. With a signalling rate of 4800 baud, it is necessary to take the 9600 bps data bits two at a time and assign them to four different carrier levels.

In more detail, a VSB transmitter consists of a data scrambler, a Grey encoder, and an amplitude signal generator. The functions of the scrambler and Grey encoder are the same as in the 208. The data pairs are then used to construct a four-level dibit waveform with the relative amplitude values of +1, -1, +3, and -3. This baseband four-level signal then amplitude modulates a 2853 Hz carrier. The carrier is suppressed and the upper sideband almost entirely removed. Since a VSB signal cannot be demodulated unless some 2853 Hz carrier is present, some carrier signal is added in quadrature to the sideband. In this sense, a VSB modem does use a quadrature amplitude modulation technique. The carrier energy is added in quadrature to ensure that it cannot cause interference or error in the demodulator. In modern VSB modems as in the QAM units, all this signal processing is done digitally, with a digital-to-analog converter providing the final line output.

71

In the receiver, an automatic gain-control circuit drives an analog-to-digital converter and the processing then becomes all digital, although we shall continue to describe what happens in analog terms. A locally generated 2853 Hz carrier oscillator is used to demodulate (frequency translate) the sideband signal to regain the baseband four-level signal. The 2853 Hz quadrature energy is filtered out and used to control the frequency and phase of a 2853 Hz carrier oscillator. Note that since both the modulated carrier and the quadrature pilot tone are transmitted together, the modem is largely immune to the effects of frequency translation in phone circuits. The 4800 baud (2400 Hz) baseband four-level data signal now goes to a sixty-tap adaptive equalizer to correct for intersymbol interference before the decision logic and descrambling. The adaptive equalizer and the 4800 baud clock recovery circuits are similar to those used in the 208 as discussed earlier.

Because of the complexity of a sixty-tap equalizer, a rather lengthy training time is usually needed. Retraining times are getting shorter, but early VSB modems took about ten seconds to train, while later ones took about three seconds. Using faster microprocessor techniques reduces this time to the 100 msec range. Unlike the 208, however, retraining in most 9600 bps modems involves both modems. A retrain cycle can be initiated manually, or when power comes on, or when RTS is raised, or when signal quality is poor. An unmodulated answer tone of, say, 2025 Hz from one modem to the other requests the training pattern and begins the training process. In a VSB modem, various signals are sent in sequence to adjust the AGC circuit, to acquire carrier phase, to acquire baud timing, to set equalizer tap coefficients and to synchronize the scrambler.

QAM Modems

Although double sideband AM modulation is inefficient, it is possible to take two AM signals and combine them without interference if one of them is in quadrature (shifted 90°) with

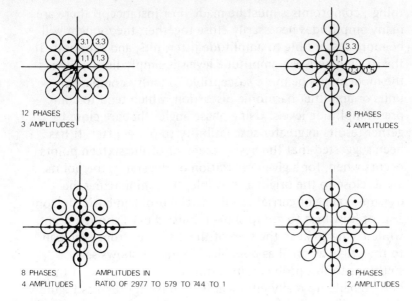

12 PHASES
3 AMPLITUDES

8 PHASES
4 AMPLITUDES

8 PHASES
4 AMPLITUDES

AMPLITUDES IN
RATIO OF 2977 TO 579 TO 744 TO 1

8 PHASES
2 AMPLITUDES

Figure 5-1/QAM Signal States Used by Different Modem Designers.

respect to the other. Furthermore, if each carrier is allowed to have four levels, the combination of the two signals will have sixteen states differing from each other in both amplitude and phase. Indeed, any combination of sixteen phases and amplitudes can be shown to be constructed from a pair of quadrature AM signals. There are as many sets of sixteen points in use as there are QAM modem manufacturers. They are distinguished by the number of different amplitudes and phases they use. For instance, one common QAM system uses twelve phases and three amplitudes (Bell 209), while others use eight phases and two amplitudes, or eight phases and four levels. In the first and last cases some combinations of phase and amplitude are illegal (see Figure 5-1).

The choice of a set of QAM points is made so as to minimize error in the presence of line impairments, but as in most things, compromises must be made. For instance, if there are many amplitudes necessarily close together, the modem will be more susceptible to amplitude jitter, hits, and dropouts. If the spacing between amplitude levels is simply linear, then the modem will be more susceptible to faulty compander units or amplifier harmonic distortion, which tend to compress amplitude levels. Using phase angles that are close together results in greater susceptibility to phase jitter. It has been suggested that the best placement of the sixteen points occurs when, for a given separation of the states, the points are as close to the origin as possible, thus minimizing the dynamic range of carrier required. The problem basically consists of how best to group sixteen billiard balls about a point while trying to keep the sum of the distances from each ball to the origin as small as possible. Figure 5-1 shows several solutions to this problem, including one where some of the billiard balls are really elliptical (C). Drawings such as Figure 5-1 are called eye patterns, and most 9600 bps modems provide voltages for the vertical and horizontal inputs of oscilloscopes so that these patterns may be viewed while the modem is actually on-line. On real lines, the points jitter about their nominal positions, and with some practice one can tell what kind of line impairments one is dealing with. If the points move radially in and out, then amplitude jitter is responsible. If the points move concentrically around the origin, then phase jitter is responsible. Random noise or jitter causes circular smearing of the points, and asymmetrical radial spreading indicates harmonic distortion. Hits and impulses will cause stray points to appear at random. Such a display is called an eye pattern, because originally, when direct displays of the carrier were used for such purposes, the various phases and amplitudes of successive superimposed carrier cycles resembled an eye, the size of whose opening was equivalent to the distance between dots on the newer displays.

74

Each manufacturer claims that his placement of points is the best; but, like the comparison between QAM and VSB, factors such as the accuracy of the adaptive equalizer, and the performance of such circuits as automatic gain control, carrier recovery, baud timing, and demodulation have more to do with the final performance of the modem than the theoretical considerations of where to place the points. Plug-in ROMs may eventually make it convenient to change QAM parameters in the field to optimize modem performance on a given leased line. Such parameters might even be controlled, much as adaptive equalizers are controlled, to automatically compute and shift to an optimum set of points.

QAM Modulation and Demodulation

The incoming data is first scrambled and then processed, four bits at a time. This means that the signalling rate is 2400 baud. However, in QAM there are two carriers in quadrature. Therefore each carrier need only be modulated with 1200 baud (1200 Hz) data. Carrier frequencies between 1700 and 1800 Hz are commonly used. The only trick in the modulator is to transform each four-bit baud (quabit?) into two modulation signals, one for each carrier, that will minimize errors in the demodulator when the signal is recovered. Grey encoding is of course one method of limiting the probability of multiple errors; another is to switch differentially among the four major quadrants of the eye pattern. Then if a phase step occurs, the demodulator can correct itself in one baud, rather than hunt for the proper reference causing errors extending over several bauds. Note that there is no simple correlation between the scrambled, Grey, and differentially encoded quabits and the modulation signals. It requires a truth table to transform the quabits into the two 1200 Hz data streams which finally modulate the carriers. Both carriers are suppressed and the final waveform occupies a bandwidth of about 2400 Hz, with no spectrum needed for pilot tones as in the VSB case.

75

In the receiver the signal is automatically gain controlled, bandpass filtered, and digitized. Let us assume for the moment that we have a source of carrier which is locked in frequency and phase to the transmit carrier. We can then use this carrier and its 90° shifted version to recover the two 1200 Hz data signals by standard AM demodulation and filtering processes. These signals then go to two separate adaptive equalizers which typically are thirty stages long. Note that in this case the equalizers remove intersymbol interference from the undecoded baseband data, rather than from the carrier, as in the 208. After equalization, the decision logic decides what the closest nominal baseband values are and then translates them to the quabit values which can then be differentially decoded, Grey decoded, and finally descrambled.

In the QAM modem, the phase error signal generated by the decision logic is used not only by the adaptive equalizer, but also by the carrier recovery circuit. The local carrier oscillator is kept in frequency synchronism by integrating the phase error signal. Since any constant error in the demodulated phase angle must be due to an error in the recovered carrier frequency, this method of carrier recovery is quite accurate and even compensates for reasonable amounts of frequency translation in the channel. The carrier phase is also kept in close adjustment by the same phase error signal.

2400 baud timing is recovered from the demodulated 1200 Hz baseband signal. Because of the scrambler, there is always a significant amount of 1200 Hz energy in the baseband signal independent of the input data stream. When a 1200 Hz signal is sampled with a 2400 bps pulse train, the samples will have their maximum amplitudes when the sampling pulse phase is such that the 1200 Hz waveform is being sampled at its 90° and 270° points. If the sampling pulse is off by 180°, the 1200 Hz waveform will be sampled at its 0 crossings and the samples will have little 1200 Hz energy. Furthermore, if

76

the energy in consecutive samples is compared, the difference will indicate in which direction the baud clock should be shifted.

The training of QAM modems is similar to that of the 208 or VSB modems. In the first phase of training, pure tones are transmitted at several frequencies to allow the AGC, carrier recovery and baud timing circuits to synchronize themselves. Then a known pattern is sent to train the adaptive equalizer, and finally a sequence is sent to synchronize the scrambler. Training periods as short as 100 msec are possible both on good lines and if the scrambler is reset instead of synchronized on data. Training on data alone may take considerably longer. When the training period is shorter than the propagation delay, such as is the case on satellite lines, it is possible to get into continuous retrain modes, where a request to train is repeated because the training pattern requested has not yet arrived. Straps to delay consecutive retrain requests can eliminate this problem.

Split Stream Options

Since the bits are modulated in parallel, four at a time, the bits may just as well originate from one, two, three or four sources. Depending on the number of bits taken per channel, data rates of 2400, 4800 or 7200 bps are possible. The systems applications of such split-stream modems and a discussion of channel clocking methods are given in Chapter Three of *Advanced Techniques in Data Communications.* *

The addition of a multiplexing facility to a 9600 bps modem does complicate some otherwise straightforward functions. For instance, a remote loopback of one channel should not loopback any of the other channels. Remote loopback is normally accomplished by sending a tone to the other end; but this method cannot be used to loop a single channel in a multiport modem, since carrier is present at all times. Thus

*Glasgal, Ralph; Dedham, MA; Artech House, 1976.

a special repetitive bit pattern must be used to initiate or terminate a remote loopback. The problem with such a feature is that, once set, it may be very difficult to clear if the line is noisy.

A common use of the multiport modem is to multiplex polling lines. If at the remote end, either a string of local terminals or a multidrop line with modems is being polled, it is necessary to transmit EIA control signals such as Request to Send and Carrier Detect. Since main channel carrier cannot be interrupted without affecting all the channels, these control signals must be sent as special patterns when data is not being transmitted. For example, when a tail-circuit modem raises Carrier Detect, the split-stream modem sends a special bit pattern to the corresponding channel at the other end, turning on the carrier detect lead to the polling device. The special bit pattern must not be outputted as data, and while the pattern is being sent it may be necessary to buffer data that is being received. When carrier goes off another pattern is sent. This time, however, at least part of the pattern may be outputted as data, since the modem has no way of knowing that channel carrier has been turned off until the pattern is complete. Thus, using a multiport modem in a polling environment may require adjustment of software to ignore the extra bits at the end of each block. The multiplexing of tail-circuit modems requires that each channel provide buffers to retime the data received from each low-speed modem, which may drift in phase or even in frequency in some systems. These buffers are usually set to their midpoints each time Carrier Detect comes on, or on powering up. Should such a buffer overflow before it is reset, three or four bits will be lost. The buffers and the control-signal propagation method described above add to the polling time, and may noticeably reduce throughput compared to an unmultiplexed system.

6

Aren't You Glad You Can Dial?

Automatic Calling Units For Computer Controlled Call Origination

The basic function of a calling unit is to do electronically for the computer what a human operator does by hand when placing a call. The steps in making a call are as follows — lift the receiver (go off-hook), wait for one or more dial tones, dial each digit, wait while the phone rings until the other end answers (or hang up if a busy signal is received or if the call is not answered within a reasonable length of time), detect a hello, and, finally, hang up at the end of the call. Fortunately, all these functions can be performed by a relatively low-cost, compact, hybrid digital and analog logic commonly referred to as an Automatic Calling Unit (ACU). The availability of such a device makes possible automatic dialing from a variety of data processing systems.

Calling Unit Applications

Computers frequently use telephone lines to transmit data. Often, they use full-time leased lines rather than dial-up lines, even though the latter may be more economical for some applications. The advantage of a dial-up approach can be seen in the following example:

A small time-sharing accounting service in Boston does a daily update of sales and inventory data for many small businesses in the Northeast area. Each of its clients is equipped with a terminal which enables the client to enter and store one or two days' transactions on a one-minute magnetic tape. After the close of business each day, the computer of the time-sharing accounting service calls each client. If data processing is not desired that day because no tape has been prepared, the computer's call is not answered by the terminal and therefore no toll is incurred. If the automatic answering terminal does answer the call, the data stored on the tape is transmitted to the computer. Later in the night, after the data has been processed, the results are returned to the terminal's printer —

again via the dial network. These calls are all made without human intervention and at a time when phone company charges are most reasonable. Communication costs have been minimized by polling the terminals via the switched network.

Such a polling system is most practical where the terminals are geographically dispersed and the connect time is relatively short. If the connect time is long, WATS lines can be used to keep costs down.

Computerized automatic dialing is used to distribute bulletins or emergency messages to remote teletypewriters or terminals; where leased-lines are used, backup in case of line failure can be provided by computer dialing of an alternate dial network connection. If all leased lines are busy, a computer can provide low-cost temporary expansion of its communications facilities in the same manner. It is possible to computer-dial via the TWX, Telex, and PBX networks as well as via the voice network.

A new feature of automatic calling devices makes it possible for a computer to dial via a leased line or through a multiplexer and a leased line (Figure 6-3). If multiplexers are used, it is possible to make multiple long-distance calls at local rates plus a share of the leased-line charge.

This kind of long-distance dialing eliminates trunk-busy problems and call completion delays, and reduces the transmission error rate. Figure 6-3 shows how a terminal user who has already manually dialed a multiplexer port can keyboard dial via a remote calling unit and reach a remote terminal. A second set of dial digits is transmitted to establish local phone connections at the remote location. This method can be used in systems where a terminal user either dials a local number or is directly connected to a remote multiplexer via leased-line facilities and a local multiplexer.

Automatic calling units are also used to contact remote data processing equipment, to monitor alarm status, or to initiate reconfiguration, loopback, or other procedures without the

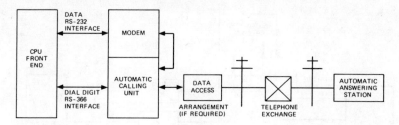

Figure 6-1/The Most Common Automatic Calling Configuration for the Polling of Remote Terminals by a Computer via the Dial Network.

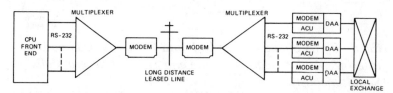

Figure 6-2/A Combination of Multiplexers and Calling Units Makes it Economical for Remote Computers to Poll via the Dial Network.

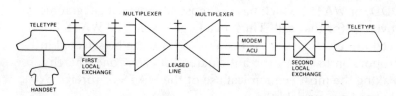

Figure 6-3/An ACU With an RS-232 Interface, and Compatible with Teletypewriter Code Makes Teletypewriter-to-Teletypewriter Dial-Up Connection via Leased Lines and Multiplexers Possible. (Note: For Clarity, not all DAAs and Modems Required in this Configuration Have Been Shown.

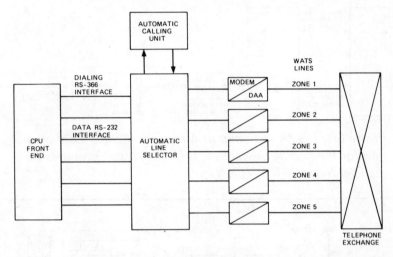

Figure 6-4/A Single Calling Unit and Computer Calling Unit Interface Adapter can Originate and Support Several Calls Simultaneously.

need to incur the cost of leased lines. An accessory phone line selector offered by at least two vendors allows a single calling unit to be shifted from one line to another (Figure 6-4). The computer can select the particular line (either local, DDD, or WATS) which has the most economical geographic coverage for that call. Thus, in a large system, all WATS lines need not cover all zones. The WATS lines can be selected in proportion to the traffic anticipated for each zone, thereby making the most economical use of the WATS or foreign exchange lines available.

To implement these and other systems, the computer must be able to interface to a dial network effectively. The balance of this chapter describes automatic calling units and other equipment that makes this marriage of a computer and the direct dial network possible.

Types of Automatic Calling Units

While most communications engineers are familiar with the EIA standard RS-232, which governs the interface between terminals, computers, and modems, the complementary EIA standard RS-366, which defines the interface between a computer and a calling unit, is less well known. The RS-366 standard defines five types of automatic calling equipment. However, there are basically only two types of calling units — one in which the numbers to be dialed are stored internally (stored number dialer); another in which the numbers to be dialed are stored in the memory of the computer. RS-366 Type I is a calling unit where single or multiple telephone numbers are stored in the unit and dialed automatically in a fixed sequence. RS-366 Type II is similar to Type I except that the computer can tell the calling unit which of the stored numbers to dial. The Type III unit is the basic ACU with which we are mainly concerned. Its most common embodiment is the 801 ACU offered by the Bell System; indeed, the RS-366 Type III specification adheres with almost no exceptions to the Bell System specification for the 801. In the 801 or RS-366 Type III automatic calling units, the phone number to be dialed is passed, a digit at a time, from the computer to the calling unit via a parallel binary coded decimal interface. (See Figure 6-5 for complete RS-366 Type III interface details.) The Type IV ACU combines a data communications device, such as a built-in modem, with the stored number dialer. The Type V equipment is not described in RS-366 at present but is meant to cover multiphone-line automatic calling equipment such as that shown in Figure 6-4 and referred to here as a phone line selector.

There are two more types not defined by RS-366. One of these is the Type VI unit (unofficial designation), which combines an 801 (Type III) with a built-in modem. Such units have the advantages of compactness and interconnection simplicity. The other is a seventh type of unit, which accepts

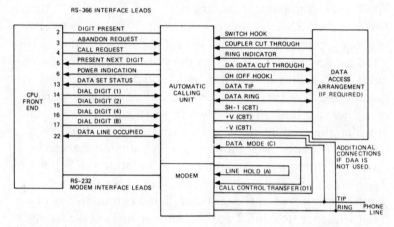

Figure 6-5/The Interface Leads Required in Normal RS-366 801-Type Dialing Systems.

dial digit information from the computer in serial form from an RS-232 interface. Implications of the serial interface are described more fully below.

Calling Unit Operation

Under straightforward RS-366 and 801 protocol, the computer indicates that it wishes to initiate a call by raising Call Request (CRQ). In response to CRQ, the calling unit goes off-hook (raises OH or if touch-tone dialing, both OH and DA, assuming a CBS or CBT data access arrangement). The calling unit then waits for dial tone and, after a fixed time-out or upon detecting the presence of dial tone or a ground on the line (if a ground start line is provided by the phone company), it sends Present Next Digit (PND) to the computer. The computer responds by putting the code for the first digit to be dialed on the NB1, NB2, NB4, and NB8 lines and then raising Digit Present (DPR). Upon sensing DPR, the

86

calling unit accepts the digit to be dialed, generates the pulses or tones required, and lowers Present Next Digit. The computer now removes DPR and the NB signals and awaits the next appearance of PND. The calling unit, after dialing the digit, pauses for the minimum interdigit time-out period and then requests the next digit of the telephone number from the computer. This process is repeated until all the digits have been dialed. The computer then either can refuse to output another digit when requested (in which case the calling unit times out and assumes the last digit has been dialed) or it can output the number 12 (End of Number, or EON) after the last digit to signify that the last number has been dialed. After EON, the calling unit may stay on the line and look for an answer tone from the answering station's modem. When the answer tone is detected, the modem is put on the line and the computer is informed that the call has been completed by raising Call Originate Status (COS) in RS-366 or Data Set Status (DSS) in the 801. The computer then may lower CRQ. After data transmission, the call normally is ended by lowering Data Terminal Ready to the modem. Should no answer be detected within a fixed time period, the calling unit sends the Abandon Call and Re-try (ACR) signal to the computer and the computer responds by lowering CRQ so that the calling unit can hang up and reset itself to try again or make a different call. A Data Line Occupied signal (DLO) is presented to the computer whenever the calling unit or the associated modem is keeping the line off-hook.

Calling Unit Protocol Variations and Options

Unfortunately, the simple scenario outlined above is merely the starting point for a seemingly infinite set of variations and options. In the paragraphs below we illustrate some of the most important of these.

There are two basic types of calling units — pulse and tone. In those sections of the country where touch-tone* dialing is

*Touch-tone is a registered trademark of AT&T.

available, the dialing time can be shortened by as much as 14 seconds per call. This time saving must be balanced against the extral cost for the line and the touch-tone dialer feature. ture.

Calling units often are used through PBX or Centrex systems which require that more than one dial tone be detected. Thus, some calling units may be strapped, or told by the computer via a control digit presented, to pause or detect dial tone not only before the first digit, but also between the first and second, the second and third, or between any digits or pairs of digits. Some calling units simply time-out for one to three seconds and assume dial tone must have arrived. Other units actually have filter detectors and detect dial tone positively, effecting a saving in the dialing time. Unfortunately, the dial tone frequencies and levels are not so uniform that this latter method can be applied throughout the country, but a combination of detection and time-out works quite well. The 801 detects the presence of central office battery rather than dial tone; therefore it has no multiple dial-tone detection feature.

Most calling units that work with computers are designed to work with modems, typically 103's or 202's. Indeed, the non-Bell calling units may be ordered with these modems built in, making possible a great savings in space, cabling, and power. Automatically answering modems of these types respond with a tone. This answer tone is recognized by the calling unit, which then tells its own modem (the originating modem) to take the line. A calling unit then needs to detect either 2025 Hz or 2225 Hz, the standard answer-tone frequencies, and also must be strappable to put the modem on the line at the beginning or the end of the answer tone. The former option is required if the modem must detect answer tone in order to handshake and put itself in the originate mode. The latter option is necessary, if the modem does not handshake, to prevent demodulation of the remainder of the answer tone and the outputting of spurious data and a premature carrier detect control signal.

Several end-of-number modes have evolved. Where the utmost speed in dialing is necessary or where a computer is chain dialing through a line selector, the relatively slow answer-tone detection process may be bypassed. The presentation of the number 12 (EON) causes the calling unit to give the line to the data set immediately. The data set must then be capable of waiting through the ringing period, handshaking if necessary, and holding the line until the call is completed.

If a computer cannot generate the number 12 code, EON operation can be simulated in some calling units by shifting control to the modem whenever a digit is not received from the computer within one second of a request. Normally, the abandon call timer is halted when answer tone is detected; however, in the EON mode the ACR timer is allowed to run out so that the computer can be interrupted to check and see if the modem is really in communication. Abandon call timers are usually adjustable from 10 to 60 s. A busy-tone detector can be used to raise ACR before the time-out has run its course. This option saves time on incompleted calls; the computer can immediately go on to the next number.

Calls can be terminated exclusively under the control of CRQ or, more normally, by a combination of CRQ and modem. The CRQ command controls disconnect until EON or answer-tone detection occurs, and the modem controls the disconnect thereafter. (Modems disconnect by detecting — loss of carrier, long space, a change in central office current, or loss of DTR). A new call should not be initiated on the same line for at least one to three seconds, to allow the central office to clear itself.

Most calling units can also answer incoming calls but must be used with modems capable of answer-mode as well as originate-mode functions.

Advanced Calling Unit Techniques

A novel computer-to-calling unit interface option eliminates the need for the rather ponderous and expensive RS-366 parallel interface. Instead, dial digits are sent serially from the computer to the calling unit via the standard EIA RS-232 communications interface ordinarily used to connect modems or teletypewriters to the computer. With this serial asynchronous data interface, dialing can be done by minicomputer, microcomputer, or, indeed, any device that outputs start-stop data, such as a multiplexer, terminal, or modem. Figure 6-6 and 6-7 show the details of such an interface; Figures 6-2 and 6-3 shows systems that can be implemented only with this type of calling unit interface — dialing is accomplished via the data channel by prefacing the data stream with the number to be dialed. The Figure 6-7 configuration is required if synchronous data is to be transmitted after dialing; all dial digits can be outputted at once and stored in the calling unit. The RS-232 control signals are used to control the call. Thus, the raising of Data Terminal Ready signifies that the com-

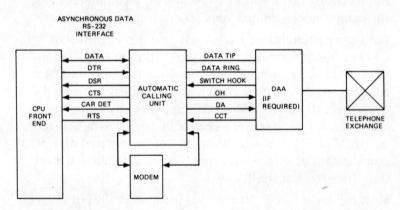

Figure 6-6/Inexpensive Single Port Dialing and Data Transmission Configuration.

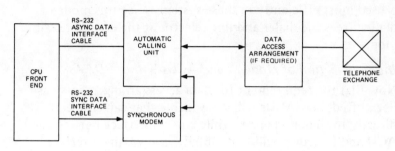

Figure 6-7/Two Port Dialing System for use with Dial-Up Synchronous Two-Wire Modems.

puter wishes to make a call. The raising of Clear to Send by the calling unit signifies that the calling unit is ready to receive the dial digit characters. A lowering of Data Set Ready by the calling unit signifies that the abandon call and re-try timer has run out.

The availability of such a simple automatic dialing interface should stimulate the development of systems built around the smaller computers in which software can be revised more easily. A line-switching unit which allows a single calling unit to dial on more than one line is shown in Figure 6-4. Such a unit is useful when the time to dial is short compared to the connect time and where many lines must be controlled. The use of a line selector eliminates not only the need for having one calling unit per line but also reduces the number of very expensive RS-366 computer ports required.

The more flexible line selectors automatically move to the next free line or are steered to a particular line by the computer. In the latter case, the first dial digit is the address of the line to be dialed on. This latter method is useful if all lines are not equal, such as when FX or zoned WATS lines are installed. Other useful features of a line selector include automatic answering and tone dialing capability. The EON option is used most efficiently in these systems since this mode of dialing frees the dialer and line selector at the earliest possible moment.

Interconnection of Modems and ACUs Without DAAs

Now that the requirement for data access arrangements has been lifted, new ACUs will be available that can connect directly to the phone line. While a new interface between an ACU and a modem will undoubtedly evolve, the interface shown as part of Figure 6-5 should remain functionally pertinent. The phone line is connected directly to both the modem and the ACU so that either unit can control the off-hook state of the line. When the ACU has finished dialing and detected answer tone or end of number, it signals the modem to hold the line by grounding the D1 line. If the modem has finished any handshaking and is not being told to disconnect by the computer, it acknowledges that it has control of the line by grounding the C contact. Then, if the computer lowers Call Request, the ACU can go on-hook without disconnecting the call. The ACU also can reset ACR when detecting the C contact. The A contact to ground tells the ACU that the modem or a handset is keeping the line off-hook, and it should raise DLO and not process any call requests.

With so many applications and types of calling units available to suit them, communications managers and systems designers should take long looks to see if all those leased lines are really necessary, and whether a marriage of multiplexers and calling units might not open up a whole new range of practical communications possibilities.

92

7

A Switch
in Line
Saves Time

Digital and Analog Switching, Patching and Monitoring Methods
Any data communications system manager with more than a
few modems, computer front-end ports, and phone lines soon
gets weary of moving cables from box to box and fighting
frayed wires and stripped threads each time a failure must be
found or a fallback configuration implemented. To eliminate
much frustration and bring order to the diagnostic or backup
process, some ten manufacturers offer a bewildering array of
switches, patch panels, relays, and monitoring arrangements.
All these products can be categorized by the basic function
each performs, the type of interface they support, and the
control method used to activate them. Purely diagnostic and
electronic network control systems are considered in the
next chapter.

Basic Switching Functions

Surprisingly, only three basic switching functions are needed
in data communications systems — bridging, interruption,
and selection (illustrated in Figure 7-1). The bridge switch
allows signals on a line to be observed without interrupting
the normal flow of signals. The line interrupt switch permits
a line to be opened for test purposes. The line selection switch
enables a line to be connected to an alternate destination.
These basic switch functions then are combined or expanded.
Figure 7-2 shows several quite useful combinations of these
basic switches. It should be understood that all switch dia-
grams shown apply to all the lines in the cables being
switched.

Multiple Switch Combinations

In addition to showing the types of basic switches, some
basic applications for these switches can be categorized. The
selector switches are used to select a modem for connection
to a terminal or vice-versa; they also can be used to connect
modems to a phone line or phone lines to a modem. Fallback
and application or computer selection are the usual reasons

95

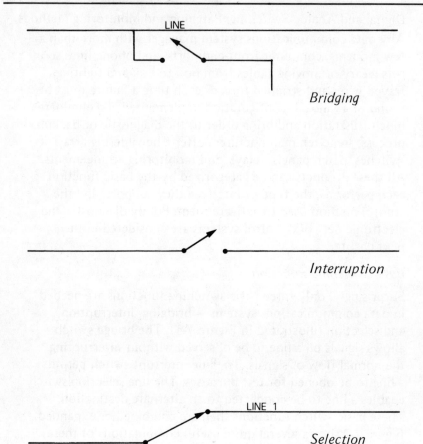

Figure 7-1/Basic Switching Functions

for installing selection switches. Figure 7-2(a) shows several selector switches which permit one line to be connected to any one of five other lines. There are EIA switches on the market with three or four positions on the same switch but, because of the number of leads involved, such switches are

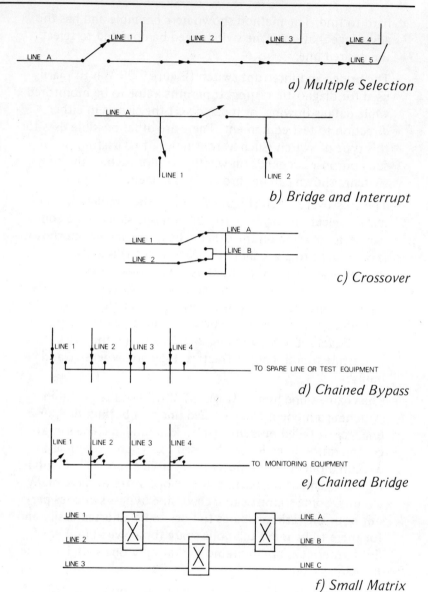

a) Multiple Selection

b) Bridge and Interrupt

c) Crossover

d) Chained Bypass

e) Chained Bridge

f) Small Matrix

Figure 7-2/Multiple and Combinational Switching Functions

hard to find. The method shown here is simple and has the advantage that only one switch need be operated to select the desired line.

The bridge and interrupt switch (Figure 7-2(b)) is primarily used for diagnostic testing. It permits a line to be monitored while data is flowing, or it can divert the signals in either direction to test equipment. There are other possible uses for this type of switch (such as routing), but its usefulness for such purposes depends on whether or not each of the three switches shown can be thrown independently.

The crossover switch (Figure 7-2(c)) is the simplest form of matrix selection switch — any line on one side can be connected to any line on the other. The crossover switch shown is equivalent to a 2 x 2 matrix; Figure 7-2(f) is a 3 x 3 matrix. A 4 x 4 matrix would use five crossover switches. While a selection matrix formed from crossover switches is relatively inexpensive, it becomes quite complex to operate. Therefore, patch panels are preferred in large-matrix applications. Several 8 x 8 switching matrices are on the market but, while functionally attractive, they are expensive and bulky.

The chained-line bypass (Figure 7-2(d)) is quite useful in switching a modem from a failed line to a backup line, or a line from a failed modem to a backup modem. The same configuration likewise can be used to switch a terminal to a backup modem or computer port, or vice versa. This switching arrangement for backup allows one spare to serve many circuits. Some sophisticated chain line bypass switches permit both the ratio of spares to lines to be adjusted easily and for there to be more than one spare for a given number of lines. Interlocks are desirable so that only one switch can be thrown at a time.

The chained-line bridge switch configuration is primarily of use where an expensive piece of diagnostic equipment is used to monitor traffic on whatever line is in difficulty. With this

98

kind of switch, no cable or line need be disturbed to connect an instrument such as an oscilloscope or meter across a line.

Basic Switching Interfaces

All the switching functions shown above can be used in switching leased lines, EIA RS-232 interface cables, wideband lines, lines to data access arrangements, or, in short, any type of data signal that can be switched safely. The number of poles a given switch requires depends on the type of line with which the switch is used. The most common places to put switches are on EIA RS-232 cables (on which 23 poles normally are provided) or on telephone lines (where 4 poles typically suffice). Not only must each switch (or patch) have the correct number of poles or contacts, it must be equipped with a proper interface connector. For EIA cables, this connector is usually a female 25-pin, although switches with any combination of male and female EIA connectors are available. Phone line switches usually are supplied with screw terminals rather than connectors. Other wideband switch types are equipped with Burndy connectors, coaxial cable connectors (BNC), or mixed coaxial and EIA connectors.

Spare Modem Switching

The most commonly used hybrid interface switch is the spare modem switch, which must interface to and switch both EIA cables and phone lines. Figure 7-3 shows how a basic switch can be chained so that one spare modem can replace any one of several on-line modems. Note that on the EIA side a double connector is required to permit the switches to be chained. Unfortunately, not all of the available manual switches on the market include this extra connector; it therefore may be necessary to chain the switches with Y cable adapters. It also should be noted that manual switch units are not interlocked, so it is possible to accidentally throw two or more switches to the spare modem position at

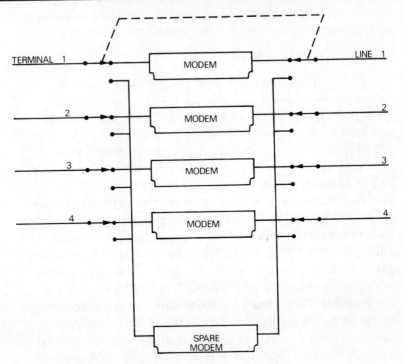

Figure 7-3/Use of Chained Bypass Switches to Switch in a Spare Modem.

the same time. However, the low cost and the reliability of this configuration make it attractive when compared to the more elaborate electrically-operated switches described below that do have interlock features to prevent such mistakes.

Switch Control

The switches described above usually are actuated mechanically, by hand. Toggles, push buttons, and knobs are all found on commercial units. Rotating knobs are probably the safest, since they are hard to actuate accidentally. Switches also can be actuated by motors, solenoids, or magnets, or they can be

100

fabricated as relays; such switches then can be actuated electrically, either locally or remotely. They also can be electrically ganged so that a whole group of switches can be activated simply by pressing a master switch. It can be a decided advantage not to have to switch 64 lines individually and by hand from one computer to a backup. It may be convenient as well to have the option to locate the master switch at the computer operator's console rather than in the communications room.

One disadvantage of several of the relay type of electrical switches on the market is that they cannot be actuated mechanically and therefore require power to operate. Should their power supply or ac power fail, the switches are frozen in position and no changes can be made until power is restored. Fortunately, a few manufacturers offer electrical switches which can be activated manually on an individual basis should power fail.

An advantage of an electronically alterable switch is that it can be controlled automatically by a computer or by a remote network control center via the dial network or other communications channel (see next chapter).

Control Signal Monitoring Switches

Most of the switch manufacturers offer their EIA switches in versions equipped with light-emitting diodes that display a few EIA control signals. While identical displays are provided by modems or multiplexers, it is convenient to have these signals displayed together in one small area. Alarm circuits are also available so that, if a signal (such as Carrier Detect) should go off, an alarm will sound. Such monitoring is inexpensive to include in switches since signal lines can be tapped easily inside the switch boxes. An auxiliary power supply usually is furnished to power the LED display.

Patching Systems

A practical, low-cost alternative to switching large numbers of lines is the patch panel. The flexibility and low cost of the patch panel is unmatched, and a single patch panel can perform any of the functions that switches can, including fallback, spare modem replacement, line bypass, line monitoring, line interruption, and, especially, matrixing. The patch panel has only one major disadvantage — it cannot be controlled remotely or ganged as electrical switches can. Some other disadvantages of patch panels are that it is necessary to use patch cords, which may be missing or damaged when needed most, and that unsophisticated operations personnel often find switches easier to use than patch fields.

Originally, the patching technique was used only with current loop lines or voice-grade lines; now patch panels are available that permit not only full 24-line EIA RS-232 patching but even wideband 50 or 56 kbps line patching. On a single patch panel or patching module it is possible to combine EIA and phone line patching. This arrangement is particularly convenient where spare modem patching is needed.

A patch panel circuit consists of two rear panel connectors and three front panel connectors. In a typical EIA RS-232 application, a computer port cable is attached to one of the rear connectors, and a cable from a modem is attached to the other. Normally the modem is connected to the computer through the patch panel wiring. One of the front panel connectors is reserved for monitoring this circuit. A piece of test equipment thus can be bridged easily across the line to monitor the traffic between modem and computer just by plugging it into the front of the panel. The other two front panel connectors are used for cross-connection of the modem or computer to other modems or computer ports. In most patch panels the insertion of a patch cord into either of these front panel connectors activates a switch which breaks the normal internal connection between the rear panel connectors, there-

102

by permitting isolated access to those lines for test or cross-connection purposes. In patch units that use EIA connectors on the front panel, a separate switch must be provided to break the normal through-connection. Patch panels that use special connectors are usually more compact and easier to use than panels that use EIA connectors, but the latter units do not require special patching cables or adapters to connect test equipment equipped with standard EIA cables.

Patch positions for pieces of test equipment, spare modems or lines can be assigned a central position on the patch panel and thereby be convenient for patching to the channel that needs backup or service. In a monitoring, test, spare modem, or spare line application, only one or two patch cables are likely to be needed. The cross-connection of two modems and two computer ports similarly requires only two patch cables.

Combination Patch Panels and Switches

In the digital-line patch panels that we have been considering, if a computer front end were to fail and it became necessary to transfer all modems or terminals to an alternate front end, one patch cable would be required for each channel and twice as many patching channels as modems would be required in order to have an appearance for each computer port. It also would be rather tiresome in a large system to have to insert or remove so many patch cables each time fallback was needed. Therefore, if fallback is involved, a patch panel with a built-in fallback switching system is preferable. Such a patching system has a third rear connector for the alternate equipment (computer, line, terminal, or modem) and a switch to select the on-line or fallback unit. This switch can be mechanical, electrical, or both. Both is the desirable option since electrical switches can be ganged and the fallback mode thereby initiated by the pressing of only one button, but mechanical switches can be thrown even if power has failed.

One common drawback to many such fallback patch panel designs is that the three front-panel connectors bridge only the on-line equipment. Therefore convenient service of the unit that has failed is impossible since it just has been disconnected from the front of the patch panel. Fortunately, more recently designed equipment provides for testing the off-line piece of equipment.

As with switches, patch panels can be equipped with lamps and alarm circuits to monitor the most important EIA control signals.

Remote Control of Switches

An advantage of electrically-actuated switches is that they can be controlled easily from remote locations thousands of miles away. The dial network is usually the most efficient means of transmitting control signals to the proper switch. A touch-tone phone used with a tone receiver-decoder offers a very inexpensive means of activating remote switches. Return tones can be utilized to confirm proper activation. ASCII-encoded signaling systems also can be utilized for such purposes.

8

The Data
Detectives

Digital and Analog Network Testing Techniques

The time when everything could best be left to IBM or the phone company is long past. The experienced data communications manager usually must assemble a system from a variety of sources in order to get the best features at the lowest possible price. It is inevitable, therefore, that sophisticated systems employ equipment from several manufacturers. When a failure occurs in such a system, it is imperative that the user be able to isolate the failure in order to call the proper repair service. One hears a great deal about finger pointing, with each vendor insisting that some other vendor's equipment is causing the problem. In truth, all the fingers should point at the Data Communications Manager, who should be willing to invest quite modest sums in the equipment that could isolate the problem before any vendor need be contacted. If you had water in your basement, you would not call a plumber to fix a hole in the roof. It is just as unreasonable to call a Bell long-lines repairperson to determine that there is no carrier on the line because the computer software is not raising Request to Send. Likewise, it is not logical to ask the IBM 3270 serviceperson to uncover the fact that excessive harmonic distortion on a leased line is responsible for a large number of negative acknowledgments. The Data Communications Department should diagnose these problems itself; with the right equipment, it's easy. In this chapter, we describe some basic types of inexpensive test equipment as well as some more sophisticated units for monitoring large systems.

The Breakout Box

The ability to get at the EIA interface leads between a terminal and a modem is essential. Several manufacturers make inexpensive breakout boxes, which allow each load in the 25-pin EIA interface to be opened, monitored, or cross-patched. Most boxes include LED lamps which indicate the activity on key clock, data, and control signal leads. Two nice

107

features to have are clock LEDs that light only if periodic transitions occur, and a lamp that indicates negative EIA voltage, so that it is possible to distinguish between a signal line that appears to be off because a line is open and one that is off because it is being held off by the terminal or modem. Rows of pins in the box make it possible to cross-connect leads or to measure them with meters and oscilloscopes.

To use a breakout box, the cable to the modem is removed and plugged into the box; the cable from the box then plugs into the modem. To avoid sex problems with some terminals, it is a good idea to have two adapter cables (male-male, and female-female) around.

Applications for breakout boxes are legion, but a few are:

1. Digital loopback external to a modem so that the cable and EIA drivers are included in the loopback test.

2. Configuring no-modems to connect terminals to terminals directly without modems.

3. Monitoring of control signals not always displayed by modems, such as reverse or secondary channel signals.

4. Monitoring CBS data access arrangements leads (requires simple cable adapters).

5. Looping receive clock to external modem clock for tail circuit applications or synchronous digital loopback tests.

6. Simulation of half-duplex protocol for modems, terminals, or computers.

Phone Line Monitor

Another piece of easy-to-use, low-cost equipment which more than pays for itself in avoided aggravation is the simple audible line monitor. A line monitor consists of an amplifier and a loudspeaker in a box with a battery and two clip leads. By bridging a phone line and listening carefully, one can determine the approximate level of the signal, whether modulation is present, a rough idea of the noise level on the line, and often whether such noise is ac hum, white noise, or impulse noise. Incidentally, the modulated carrier of modems sounds like white noise, a rushing sound like that heard between stations on an unmuted FM radio. Asynchronous 103- and 202-type modems produce pure tones if they are marking or spacing continuously. The line monitor also can be used to determine quickly if a 103 modem is in an originate or answer mode. More elegant speaker monitors include a decibel meter, which quantifies the line level more exactly and which can monitor line impairments in the presence of a holding tone (see below).

Phone Line Analyzers and Simulators

Leased lines are prone to a variety of impairments that affect the ability of modems to transmit data without error. Before discussing how these impairments can be detected and measured, we list and describe them. First, there are line defects that modulate any carrier signal put on the line, such as dropouts; frequency, phase, or amplitude jitter; and amplitude or phase hits. Sources of these line disturbances include Doppler shift, fading, hum modulation in amplifiers or oscillators, noisy modulators, power transients, and lightning. These impairments can generate unwanted carrier sidebands at virtually any frequency between 300 and 3000 Hz. Note that, in the absence of a carrier or test tone (holding tone), these defects are not detectable.

Harmonic distortion in amplifiers and compandors is another type of disturbance which is only detectable when tone is present. Frequency translation is a characteristic of frequency-multiplexed phone lines. Such channels are shifted up in frequency for transmission via cable or microwave and then shifted down for local delivery; if the shifting is not symmetrical, a residual offset is left, typically 1 to 8 Hz. Thus, a transmitted 1000 Hz tone arrives as 1008 Hz. Line impairments which are present even when no signal is on the line include impulse noise, white noise, and single frequency interference such as hum or crosstalk.

109

Short-term modulations of the signals on lines are called hits or dropouts. These are abrupt changes in the amplitude, phase, or frequency of the signal. There are both slow and fast hits and dropouts, as well as noisy dropouts. Some line impairments are caused by the pulse code modulation equipment used by the phone company to digitize analog signals prior to multiplexing, such as quantizing noise, timing errors, compandor mistracking, and foldback modulation products.

All these different types of line impairments affect modems in different ways. Some modems are insensitive to frequency translation but very sensitive to harmonic distortion, and vice versa. To select the best modem for a given application, some idea of the type of private line to be supplied should be obtained from the phone company. For instance, if the line is to be pulse-code modulated and then time-division multiplexed, it will not suffer any frequency translation; therefore, a modem with relatively poor resistance to frequency translation but high resistance to amplitude distortion and phase jitter would be superior in this application to one that does well in the presence of frequency translation but is only average in regard to other line impairments.

Obviously, selecting the right type of modem for a given application requires a piece of test equipment that can generate each type of line impairment. Several brands of modems then can be tested and their error rates compared as each line impairment is generated. Several types of such line simulators are on the market; the better ones permit the carrier signal from a modem to be modulated in frequency and amplitude over a wide range of rates, frequency translated up and down, distorted symmetrically and asymmetrically, and modulated by pulses in amplitude and phase. Most line simulators also provide calibrated amounts of white noise, impulse noise, and single-frequency energy to mix with the carrier signal.

The signal from the modem is connected first to the line simulator, which modifies it and puts it through a network

110

or cable the frequency and delay responses of which are typical of an average phone line. The final output then goes to the same modem's receiver or to another modem. Test patterns sent around the loop are used to determine the error rate. There are pitfalls to be avoided in this type of testing, however. For instance, some sophisticated modems are able to detect when they are on bad phone lines and, as the error rate increases, at some arbitrary threshold they automatically stop demodulating, clamp their receivers, and, in some cases, enter a retrain mode. If possible, all such automatic signal quality detection features should be disabled before comparative tests are run; otherwise, the tests only determine the arbitrary line quality threshold settings of the modems.

The question still remains, however, as to how one detects and measures these line impairments on actual phone lines in order to determine whether a given modem can function on a line or to explain to the phone company specifically what is wrong with the line. Over the years, many different types of meters and counters have been put on the market to measure distortion, to count hits or impulses, or to display frequency components. The cost and complexity of this type of equipment is probably not justified even for large installations, unless an engineer is available to use the equipment and interpret the results. Furthermore, rms, counting, or integrating instruments; eye pattern data quantizers; and even automatic equalizer setting analyzers overlook important transient phenomena, incorporate arbitrary threshold parameters, and cannot respond to combinational effects or new line impairments that crop up as new network equipment is designed.

Acting on the principle that a good picture is worth a thousand numerical readings, Frank Bradley of Bradley Telcom Corp. has engineered a most ingenious line analysis technique. He has made possible the uncovering of several previously undetectable line impairments, such as slow phase hits and slowly varying delay distortion. A Bradley Line Analyzer looks at a line in very much the way a modem does. A tone, say

111

1000 Hz, is put on the line to be tested. At the other end of the line, the signal consists of this tone plus all the noise and modulation components added by the line. The Bradley Line Analyzer locks onto the 1000 Hz tone and subtracts it from the total signal, leaving a residue called "normalized notched noise." The residue then is displayed on a cathode ray tube in phaser form such that vertical deflection represents the amplitude of the residue, and horizontal deflection indicates its phase angle with respect to the carrier. This type of vector display is exceptionally versatile and easy to interpret, in comparison to time- or frequency-domain displays. Relatively inexpert personnel can make a thorough line test in a minute or so, either by a glance at the pattern on the screen or by listening to the built-in loudspeaker which provides an acoustical replica of the predominant line impairments. For instance, phase hits sound like pings, impulse noise like clunks, and amplitude or phase modulation like two tones spaced by the modulation frequency. Specific line impairments are likewise quite easily identifiable by the patterns they produce on the CRT screen. Each type or combination of impairments has its own look; with only a little practice, one can identify not only line impairments but also the type of transmission facility used. For instance, in FDM channel banks, phase jitter and therefore horizontal deflection predominates. Multilobed patterns indicate harmonic distortion; deflection off the vertical and horizontal axes indicate noise or, if circular around the origin, single frequency interference.

By using such a line analyzer, it is possible to determine in advance whether a given line can support 9600 bps transmission. For instance, if it is known that, for a given modem, a phase shift of 22.5° will cause an error, it is possible to examine the analyzer display for a few minutes to see if the horizontal deflection (and therefore the sum of phase jitter, random noise, harmonic distortion lobes, etc.) ever exceeds 22.5° in one direction. If a line problem does arise, such an instrument makes it possible to tell the phone company exactly what the problem is in a language phone company technicians can understand. Special options permit remote diagnosis of line segments from a central site via the dial network; the required carrier tones are injected automatically at the ends of the lines being analyzed.

Error Rate Tester

Bit or block error testers are useful in determining whether a given modem and line are functioning properly. Error-rate tests are made via the EIA interface by putting a modem or its line in a loopback condition, sending a known pattern, and then checking the looped pattern for errors. Many synchronous modems have such pattern generators and error detectors built-in. Error checking of asynchronous modems usually requires an external tester. One must be careful, though — many so-called asynchronous pattern generators do not actually generate characters with start and stop bits, and therefore may not be suitable for use in testing equipment such as multiplexers, buffers, code converters, printers, etc. They are, however, suitable for testing all modem types except for some full-duplex 1200 baud ones that are character structure sensitive.

Most error-rate testers also include some of the EIA line monitoring and biasing facilities found in the EIA breakout boxes described above. Despite the popularity of these testers, it can be argued that error-rate testing is of limited value since computers, terminals, multiplexers, and even modems seldom fail in ways that would produce random errors. Digital equipment failures are usually catastrophic, or at least systematic. Thus, error testers are really line quality measuring devices of a rather primitive type, since they do not indicate specifically what is wrong with a line.

One interesting application for an error-rate tester occurs when a dial network connection is established. In this case it is desirable for the caller to know if a connection is really good before sending a great deal of data. However, two-wire

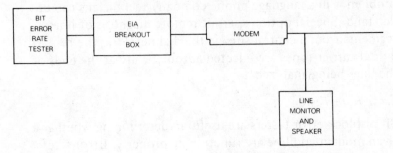

Figure 8-1/Interconnection of Typical Test Equipment

lines with half-duplex modems cannot be looped; therefore, the usual error testers cannot be used unless there are two of them and an assistant is at the other end. What can be used in this case is a pair of special error-testing devices (available from at least one manufacturer, circa mid-1977). A master unit turns on carrier and sends a special pattern to a slave unit at the remote end, which counts the errors and sends the error count and a second test pattern back to the master which displays the error count for the round trip. If the line is good enough so that redialing is not necessary, both the master and slave testers become transparent to data, and transmission proceeds.

Digital Protocol Monitors and Terminal Simulators

The most sophisticated of the data detectives discussed in this chapter is the protocol monitor and simulator, available from any of a number of different manufacturers. Most of these devices resemble CRT terminals; their primary application is in the debugging of new communications software and transmission formats and newly-installed hardware rather than in the routine diagnosis of phone line or modem failures once a system is functioning properly. There are some timing and control signal problems in communications links that can be analyzed quite expeditiously using just a data monitor.

114

The protocol monitor bridges the EIA interface between a terminal and a computer or modem. In some cases, a spare terminal can be used as a monitor by bridging it across the line using a "T" cable adapter; however a unit specifically designed for monitoring can display both send and receive data, and include in the display an indication of when Carrier Detect, Request to Send, and Clear to Send come on in relation to the data. Underlining, line labeling, reverse video, and dim and bright attributes are set to distinguish between send and receive modes and between data and control characters. Most monitors actually cannot display send and receive data simultaneously, but count on the fact that most protocols are half-duplex, and send and receive data alternate. Special options from a few manufacturers permit true full-duplex operation and compatibility with new protocols (such as SDLC), by either alternating lines in the display, marking the lines as send and receive, or splitting the screen. Display screen sizes vary from one character to 1,920. The units also contain buffer memories of varying sizes, allowing off-line searches through large amounts of stored data. Tape storage options on nearly all the units permit nonvolatile storage of up to a half-million characters. However, for ordinary use, such mass storage is tedious to search and usually is not needed.

Two features of the better monitors effectively reduce the need for tape storage. One is an idle character delete option that allows the storage and display of just the actual data characters. Since idle time predominates in most systems, this condensation is quite effective in conserving display and memory buffer space. At times, though, it is useful to store and display idle characters in order to determine the turn-around time or the time between polls. The second feature that helps to use storage efficiently is a programmable trap — a circuit that starts the storage when a particular event or character sequence occurs. Some examples include starting to record when Carrier or Clear to Send comes on, a parity error occurs, or a NAK is received. The trap can be set to preserve characters before the event as well as after it so that both the cause and the effect can be observed.

The better monitors can monitor asynchronous or synchronous data and have provisions for setting the block synchronization character or characters to the patterns used in a particular format. The CRTs usually display characters as text or in hexadecimal form; special patterns are used to display control characters such as ETX or carriage return. Most monitors also include an EIA interface signal display and have the capability for patching the EIA signals to the event trap circuits so that a control signal or data transition can trigger memory retention or stop the recording process.

While monitors are quite useful in locating problems in new systems that need debugging, simulators are often indispensible in getting new systems on-line quickly. A good simulator can mimic virtually any terminal or computer format. It is a significant advantage to be able to exercise a new terminal even when computer time is not available, or to test computer software before a new terminal has arrived. Simulators are essentially monitors with transmission capabilities and a keyboard. The keyboard is used to enter or program the variable elements of a given protocol, such as data format (code, speed, parity, async, sync, etc.), polling interval, RTS-CTS delay, RTS turnoff delay, transmission delay, sync character format, polling message, and terminal response message. To avoid having to enter all this data each time the simulator is used, the basic parameters can be stored in nonvolatile storage (ROMs); the keyboard is used to make small modifications when necessary. Simulators differ primarily in the variety and complexity of the messages and responses they can store and interpret. Thus, if you anticipate simulating a computer polling sixteen remote terminals, be sure that the simulator can accommodate the required number of polling sequences. Since it is tedious to enter long, complex programs from the keyboard or to wait for new ROMs to be

116

made, some simulators permit the loading of programs and protocols from external units such as computers or cassettes.

Most simulators also include modem and line error-rate measuring features identical to those found in the much lower cost error-rate testers discussed earlier. An advantage of monitoring an error-rate test is that the exact nature of the error can be observed in some units, rather than just getting a count of how many errors occur. It is often useful to know whether errors are random or systematic — if random in both time and type, the transmission line is probably at fault; if systematic in type, the computer, terminal, or modem is at fault. Periodically repeating errors usually indicate a synchronous-modem problem, while errors that affect a particular bit in a character (such as a start or a parity bit) are almost always the fault of a terminal, computer or TDM.

In summary, if only the identification of a catastrophic failure in an already working network is required, a monitor or simulator is probably "overkill." The simple test equipment described earlier and the network monitoring systems to follow are much more efficient in pinpointing catastrophic failures in formerly working systems than are monitors. However, if a new network is to be debugged, or new software and hardware are to be tested, a monitor-simulator may well prove indispensable. Note that monitors and simulators usually are used by technically sophisticated personnel (programmers and engineers), while the other items described in this chapter are more useful for operational personnel involved in routine maintenance or field service.

Network Control Systems

Some special diagnostic problems exist in multipoint polling networks. For example, suppose that one terminal on an eight-terminal line has failed in such a manner that it keeps on Request to Send, causing the associated modem to hold its carrier on all the time and thus preventing reception of modulated carrier signals from other polled locations. At the

117

central site, the computer operator may notice that receive carrier is always on, but there is no simple way to determine which of the eight remote terminals is responsible for the abnormal condition. Normal modem loopback diagnostics do not function in this situation. Furthermore, there seldom is anyone at any of the eight remote sites equipped to assist the central-site operator in running diagnostic tests and restoring service. Even with remote help, the central-site operator would have to contact each remote site in turn, and the system likely would be down for an hour or more. This kind of failure is called "streaming," and virtually all of the independent modem manufacturers have developed multipoint network control systems to solve this and other two-point and multipoint network control problems.

A typical network control system consists of a central control console and a responder at each remote site. The central control unit can be microprocessor-controlled, and the operator can interface to the control unit via either a standard CRT terminal with keyboard or a custom-designed display panel of switches, lamps, and digital number readouts. The responders are either cards that receive and respond to commands from the central control and which are built into a specific brand of remote modem, or external remote units that can be used with any brand of modem or with DDS service units. In many cases, a given network control system works only with modems of the same manufacturer.

In-Band Network Control

The least expensive approaches to centralized point-to-point and multpoint network control are illustrated in Figures 8-2 and 8-3. The remote units wrap around the modems and monitor the receive digital data stream for special patterns that represent diagnostic commands from the central controller. Functions such as line loopback, remote digital loopback, and error-rate testing can be performed entirely from a central site with relatively inexpensive equipment. Restoral

118

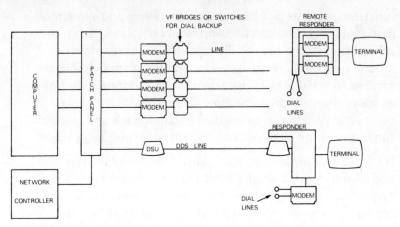

Figure 8-2/Network Control System for Point to Point
Configuration

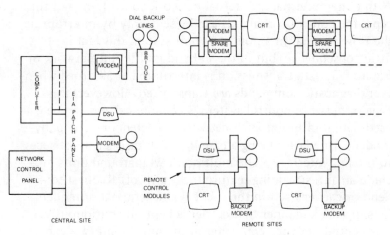

Figure 8-3/Multipoint Network Control System Using
In-Band Signalling Techniques

119

functions, such as dial backup and spare-line and spare-modem switching, also can be controlled completely from the central site. In the case of dial backup, each remote wraparound unit contains autoanswer circuitry that switches the modem to the dial network when the two phone lines ring at approximately the same time. Note that such a central diagnostic system can be used to add loopback and restoral functions to the DDS network which otherwise lacks them.

It should be pointed out that many point-to-point synchronous modems have similar built-in remotely controllable diagnostic features, but none that we know of offers self-contained remote-controlled restoral features. When the diagnostics are built into the modem, it is not possible to perform diagnostics from one central site control panel — one must go to each modem itself to run tests. Another disadvantage of built-in modem loopback diagnostics is that digital loopback usually does not test the EIA interface circuits — a relatively common source of failure.

With either external or internal network control units of this type, the control commands can be sent only by interrupting the flow of data. In a point-to-point system this fact is of little consequence, but in the in-band multipoint network of Figure 8-3, data transmission is interrupted at all drops whenever diagnostic commands are transmitted. However, this type of network control system is economical and can be used with multipoint DDS networks or telephone company modems (the latter being a case in which tariffs restrict access to the line interface). The multipoint wraparound units include an anti-streaming feature that turns off Request to Send or carrier itself in the event that a terminal or modem fails in such a manner that carrier is kept on continuously. The central network controller in the multipoint case can select which remote drop it wishes to test; each remote wraparound unit is strapped to respond only to its own address code.

120

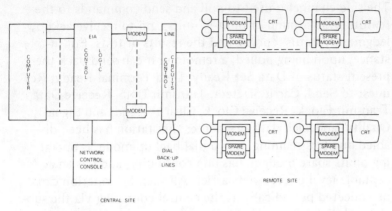

Figure 8-4/Multipoint Network Control System Using Out-of-Band Signalling Techniques

Out-of-Band Multipoint Network Control

In order to monitor or test a particular drop on a multipoint line without interrupting the flow of data to the other points in the network, it is necessary to transmit the control network commands and responses in a manner that does not interfere with the main data channel. This transmission can be done inexpensively by a form of frequency division multiplexing. In essence, the controller and the remote units communicate over a part of the line not used by the modems of the main data channel. The region between 300 and 400 Hz is usually safe to use for such a purpose if a slow asynchronous data rate, such as 75 baud, is used. Figure 8-4 shows how a single central control console can monitor an entire network having many lines and drops without any mechanical switching or patching being required. The address of the line and drop to be tested is selected via thumbwheel switches from the console. In the case of the more sophisticated units, the controller can be set to scan automatically all drops and lines in sequence, setting an alarm when something abnormal is found.

The side channel is used to poll and send commands to the remote wrap-around or built-in units, and to receive acknowledgments, status reports, and the results of tests. For instance, upon being polled, a remote unit can send back the present status of Data Set Ready, Data Terminal Ready, Request to Send, Carrier Detect, Transmit Data, Receive Data, Transmit Clock, Receive Clock, Clear to Send, and Signal Quality, and such data as whether the station has been disabled due to streaming, is in a dial backup mode, is operating on its spare modem, has line continuity, and has an acceptable level of received carrier. All such information can be collected periodically at the central controller via the subchannel without any interference with normal data transfer. Automatic scanning for such abnormal conditions as Data Terminal Ready off, Data Set Ready off, Carrier Detect off, or no acknowledgment of a subchannel request for status makes it possible to detect most any failure almost at the instant it occurs. Such a failure discovery is followed by the sounding of an alarm and the display of the alarm condition with the time and location of the failure.

Once a failure has been detected and isolated to a particular drop, quite a few tests can be run without interference with other drops on the same line. Such noninterfering diagnostic or restoral functions include switching to a standby line or modem, going to dial-backup, and executing a modem self-test. In the latter test, a modem at the remote drop is disconnected from the line and looped on its analog side through an appropriate attenuator. A test pattern then is fed to its digital input by the wrap-around unit, and the receive data is checked for errors. The results of this test then are sent to the central controller for display. Other on-line diagnostic functions include the turning on or off of modem carrier, and the enabling of an automatic anti-streaming feature (based on a maximum permissible time for Request to Send to be on).

Off-line functions that interrupt data traffic to all drops include local and remote loopbacks, error-rate testing, and polling tests, all performed at the main channel data rate. It is rare, however, that on-line scanning and testing via the subchannel does not locate the problem first.

Most network control systems also permit testing lines on the far side of multiplexers, split-stream modems, or remote concentrators; special controllers relay their commands and responses around these devices. With such a relay system, it is quite feasible for an operator in New York to diagnose a problem and restore service on a multidrop line between Los Angeles and San Francisco. Other features of an elaborate network control system include periodic maintenance reports and a printed log of alarm conditions.

9

That Old Black Box Magic

In this chapter, several gadgets are described which are rather ingenious solutions to some common data communications system problems. All the devices are connected between a terminal or computer and its modem, and operate on the digital data stream to provide compatibility, to improve throughput, or to enhance security.

Asynchronous to Synchronous Data Converters

One of the basic tenets of data communications is that long-distance transmission of asynchronous data over voice-grade lines is limited to data rates of 1800 baud or less. However, there are many asynchronous terminals that operate at speeds such as 2400, 4800, and 9600 baud. Most such terminals are colocated with their computers, but quite often a need arises to use them remotely. A Hobson's choice then must be made whether to cut speed to 1800 or 1200 baud, or to replace the terminals with more expensive synchronous terminals that can run faster but which require new front-end hardware and software support.

An inexpensive solution to this problem is the asynchronous-to-synchronous converter. Such a device receives the characters asynchronously by looking for the start bit, and stores the characters in a buffer so that the modem can clock them out usually including their start and stop bits, with its send clock. The same device can be used to couple asynchronous terminals to the DDS network.

The data as finally transmitted by the modem or DSU is isochronous, synchronous, and asynchronous all at the same time. Thus the synchronous data received by the synchronous modem or DSU can go directly into the asynchronous terminal without conversion. There are, though, some precautions that must be observed when using such converters. If the asynchronous terminal is slower than the synchronous modem (as when an 1800 baud terminal is put on a 2400 bps DDS line), the converter buffer empties faster than it can be filled and a buffer-full condition never occurs. If, however,

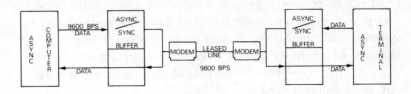

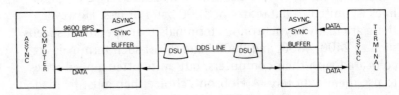

Figure 9-1/Asynchronous data transmission at rates up to 9600 bps are possible using simple conversion unit on synchronous lines.

a 2400 baud terminal is put on a 2400 bps line, data may accumulate in the buffer if the asynchronous clock is slightly faster than the synchronous clock. Eventually the buffer will overflow and data will be lost. To prevent this occurrence, the asynchronous data should be generated with periodic pauses to allow the buffer to empty. For example, if the clock speed difference is .05%, one character will be accumulated for every 2000 transmitted. If a four-character buffer is provided, 8000 characters can be transmitted head to tail without pause before an error will occur. In normal systems, buffer overflow is seldom a problem. A Request to Send stretching circuit prevents the lowering of Request to Send to the modem before the buffer is emptied.

Error Control

One disadvantage of using high-speed asynchronous terminals at remote locations (such as in Figure 9-1) is that there is usually no error control. Since the system probably was designed with only local terminals in mind, transmission error control was not needed and provisions were not made for it. The most common way of getting around this problem (getting a bisync or SDLC terminal, new front end, and software support) is expensive and time consuming. The alternative is quite simple in concept. Use an error control black box between the terminal and modem, as shown in Figure 9-2. In this manner, most of the advantages of the synchronous block transmission formats can be obtained at a fraction of the cost and without modifications to terminal or software.

There are basically two types of error control — retransmission of data received in error (ARQ) and correction of errors by the receiver (Forward Error Correction, or FEC). The ARQ type of error control unit takes data from the terminal, formats it into blocks, and adds a header and check bits at the beginning and end of each block, respectively. A relatively small number of check bits allows detection of virtually all types of errors in a block. When a block is found to be in error, a request is made for retransmission of the block. Data throughput is determined primarily by the number of blocks that must be retransmitted. Additional time may be lost in formats such as bisync that require that each block be acknowledged as correct before the next block is sent. The new Synchronous Data Link Control (SDLC) eliminates the time lost in waiting for the acknowledgments by sending acknowledgments while subsequent blocks are sent; however, SDLC cannot make up for the loss of throughput due to noisy lines, nor can any other ARQ system. Thus, ARQ, if applied to a 9600 bps modem link operating with a burst error rate of one burst of errors in every 10,000 bits and having blocks of 3000 bits, would result in a throughput of only 5,568 bps,

127

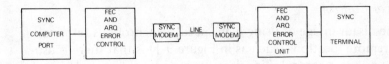

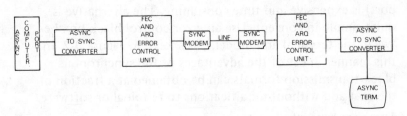

Figure 9-2/Error control units improve throughput and may eliminate the basic need for elaborate error control protocols such as sole or bisync.

because some 42% of the blocks would need to be retransmitted. At this rate, a 4800 bps modem might as well be used to save some money and eliminate many of the errors.

Thus ARQ or bisync is not always the best answer to error control for modems, multiplexers, or terminals that do not already include error control; forward error control has some real advantages in such situations. By adding some 140 check bits to a block of 4000 bits, it is possible not only to detect but also to correct for burst errors up to 50 bits wide. On real lines well over 90% of the errors that occur can be corrected.

In a real system, though, 100% correction is desired. The answer is to request the retransmission of the few uncorrected blocks and to combine FEC and ARQ techniques so as to optimize the throughput. In the combined ARQ-FEC units

128

available today, it is possible to improve the error rate by a factor of 10^6 at an overhead cost of only 15%. Thus, a 9600 bps modem on a 10^{-4} line could deliver 8160 bps with an error rate of 10^{-10}. The 1,440 overhead bits actually need not be lost if it is considered that, with the exception of a few sync characters, the terminal in theory need not waste any bits on protocol or check characters of its own. The throughput can be enhanced further if the error control units use a full-duplex method similar to SDLC to acknowledge correct blocks or to request retransmission of wrong blocks. Note that, on occasion, as in any ARQ system, if too many retransmissions occur in a given period of time, the buffers of the transmitting unit may fill up. Therefore, there must be a mechanism to halt temporarily the flow of data from the terminal or computer. For asynchronous terminals, a lowering of Clear to Send may be adequate; for synchronous terminals, an interruption of the send clock may be permissible.

FEC can be used to advantage with TDMs. By using smaller block sizes, delay in the error control system can be held to less than 100 ms. The error control unit must clock the multiplexer, however, and therefore the multiplexer must be of a type not sensitive to the fact that the clock supplied is nominally 15% less than each of the standard modem clock rates of 2400, 4800, and 9600 bps.

Increasing Throughput of Batch Terminals on Satellite Lines

New satellite leased lines are attractive for data communications because of their lower cost, higher reliability, and sometimes wider bandwidths than typical domestic or international terrestrial circuits. However, the propagation delay on such a circuit is typically a third of a second. Thus a terminal using a half-duplex block transmission protocol, such as bisync, would have to wait two-thirds of a second to find out if the last block it sent was received properly. If 5,000-bit blocks were being sent at 9600 bps, more than half the time would

129

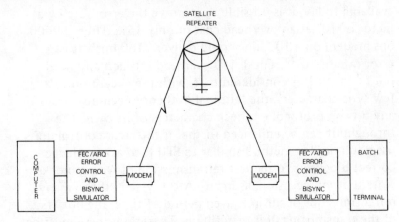

Figure 9-3/Elimination of Satellite Delay Effect on Through-put by Error Control and Protocol Simulation

be spent in waiting; the throughput might be as low as 2400 bps if retransmissions due to errors were taken in to account.

The system could be converted to a protocol such as SDLC that was designed to avoid this problem, but a much more convenient solution is to use the ARQ/FEC box described above in combination with a bisync protocol simulator. The final satellite error control unit works as follows. After a terminal has been polled by the computer, it outputs a block of data to the satellite error control unit, which gives back an immediate acknowledgment. The terminal then can begin immediately to release the next block of data. The first block meanwhile is formatted, transmitted, forward error corrected (or ARQed, if necessary), and delivered to the remote computer without error. The computer's acknowledgment is then ignored. On those rare occasions when too many blocks need retransmission, the terminal can be given a negative acknowledgment to keep it from outputtting data until the backlog is cleared.

130

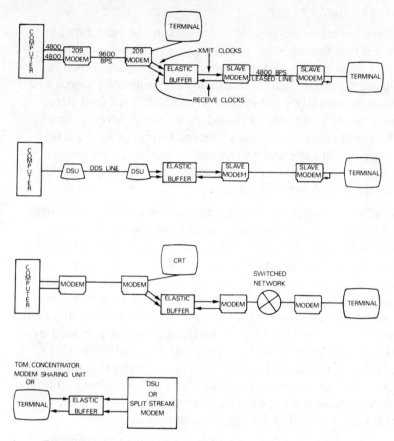

Figure 9-4/Applications of the Elastic Interface Unit

Any batch transmission protocol can be fooled in this manner, and improvements in throughput of 300% have been observed. The shorter the batch block and the faster the data rate, the greater the improvement. This technique is not as suitable, though, for multidrop systems using polling protocols. In such systems, one still must wait for the response to a poll from each controller or terminal; therefore the improvement in throughput is smaller, depending on the ratio of polls to data blocks.

Elastic Interface Unit

There are many times when it is necessary to feed data between two synchronous devices, one of which cannot be clocked externally. Some common examples are shown in Figure 9-4; they include the analog extension of a digital network such as DDS, the extension of unbuffered split-stream modems or synchronous time-division multiplexer channels, the connection of internally clocked terminals to the DDS network or to the second channel of a split-stream modem, and any half-duplex extension of DSUs, modems, or TDMs (such as a dial network link).

The basic problem in all these applications of the elastic interface unit is that the data crossing the interface is not in step with the clock that is asking for it. In the case of a dial network extension, even the data rates may be different. In particular, a DSU asks for data to transmit on pin 2 by outputting a transmit clock on pin 15. If this data is receive data from a modem, it emerges from pin 3 of the modem at a rate and phase determined by the receive data clock provided by the modem on pin 17. An elastic interface buffer for this application must accept data into a register using the modem clock on pin 17, then allow the DSU clock on pin 15 to remove it from the register. The buffer also twists the data leads so as to match data inputs and outputs.

Since the elastic interface buffer is a relatively inexpensive device, it usually only buffers eight bits or less. Its buffer is set to the midpoint when power is turned on; in the better units, the buffer is also reset to its midpoint when modem carrier comes on. This option is only significant in the dial network extension case in which the modem receive clock at the remote end of the line cannot be used as an external send clock. Thus, it would be possible for the buffer to underflow or overflow if it were not reset, preferably at the start of each new block of data.

132

Figure 9-5/Data scramblers prevent theft or spoofing of data.

Usually one channel of a split-stream modem can accept an
external clock. Therefore the extension circuit modem or
DSU can be connected to this port directly if a properly
twisted cable adapter is used. However, if two or more tail
circuits have to be driven from the same split-stream modem,
the buffer units must be used on the second or subsequent
lines if the modem port is unbuffered or cannot accept an
external clock.

Data Encryption

There are many data communications systems these days in
which theft by someone tapping a phone line is a very real
possibility. Such sensitive applications include credit card
transaction verification, electronic fund transfer, cash dis-
pensing machines, and confidential financial data processing.
Fortunately, putting data scramblers as close to the outputs
of terminals and computers as possible (see Figure 9-5) is a
relatively inexpensive way to prevent theft or spoofing by
someone tapping phone lines or EIA cables.

A data scrambler consists of a random bit generator which,
when digitally combined with data, produces an encrypted
data stream (cipher) that appears to be completely random.
The decryption unit generates an identical random bit pattern, which is subtracted from the encrypted stream to recover the original data.

The trick in data encryption is to make such a pseudo-random pattern, or key as it is called, so long and complicated
that a thief — even with the aid of the fastest computer in

133

existence — could not unscramble the message in a period of time short enough for the information recovered still to be of value. Many of the techniques used to generate keys are confidential, but a key usually is formed in a long shift register. The bits entering or passing through the shift register are modified by feedback from the end or several intermediate stages. By providing switches to change the feedback points, the key can be varied — which should be done at regular intervals to provide additional security. Sophisticated encryption units put an additional level of logic in the feedback paths to make the feedback nonlinear; that is, the state of one feedback signal influences the feedback to another point in the register, either at that instant or several clock cycles later. A modern key generator typically can develop 4,000 trillion different pseudo-random key patterns with key lengths of up to 10^{52} bits. Another feature of data scramblers which enhances security is a random start capability, so that the key does not always begin at the same point each time power is applied or transmission initiated.

From the communications standpoint, there are several important factors to consider. First, data scramblers must be synchronized to each other because the descrambler must know exactly what portion of the key to use to decrypt the message. There are two methods of synchronizing key generators. In the first, a synchronization pattern is sent to initialize the descrambler. Thus, every time transmission is begun, a synchronization preamble must be sent ahead of the data. The disadvantage of this type of synchronization is that, if synchronization is lost due to noise or clock drift, recovery is not automatic and a considerable amount of data may be lost before resynchronization occurs. In polling systems, the resynchronization delay can increase the polling time substantially. However, an advantage of this technique is that simple transmission errors after synchronization are not multiplied in the decryption process.

134

The second synchronization method is an inherent part of the encryption scheme. If the data itself is passed through the shift register that generates the key, the data history is an element in the formulation of the key. The decryption device then becomes self-synchronizing — if enciphered data passes through the register in the decrypter, it eventually contains the exact pattern that the encrypting register did, and the registers therefore must come into lockstep. This technique eliminates the need for transmitting the key starting point; therefore, it yields less information to the thief.

The key pattern, being dependent on data, seldom repeats and is not determined solely by the feedback switch settings, which could be compromised. Attempts to modify encrypted messages en route (e.g., to change dollar amounts or account numbers) result in improper decryption because the data history is not correct. Any synchronization error is corrected automatically as more enciphered data is sent. However, transmission errors are multiplied — single bit errors usually garble the next four or five characters. The data encrypter automatically delays Clear to Send to the terminal until after synchronization is assured.

There are both synchronous and asynchronous data scramblers. In the synchronous case, all the data bits usually are enciphered so that the data scrambler need not be protocol sensitive. Where packet switching or satellite turn-around-delay elimination techniques are used, it may be necessary to leave some header characters unencrypted. For asynchronous data, it is usually the practice to leave unencrypted all control characters, such as carriage return, line feed, shift, and break signal. The encryption unit also monitors its own cipher to ensure that the data characters it encrypts do not look like such control characters. If transmission is asynchronous, the start-stop bits also must be left intact. It is possible, though, to encrypt start and stop bits if the stop bits are made integral so that clock can be recovered from the data stream to clock the decoder.

Another useful feature of asynchronous systems is a remote switching feature to shift a receiver automatically from clear to the encrypted mode. This transition is done by sending an impossible data character combination, such as QQ or KK, which causes the remote end to shift its mode. It is also possible in some encryption equipment to change the code settings electronically rather than manually. In such systems it is possible for a computer to determine — randomly and without operator knowledge — the particular key to be used to transmit data. The commands to change the key at the remote end are encrypted using the previous key setting, thereby insuring maximum protection.

Conclusion

There are, of course, many other black boxes that from time to time are quite useful; among these are the interface and code converters. Boxes are available to convert from EIA RS-232 to current loop, military standard, or any of various European CCITT or wideband interfaces. Also available are units that convert Baudot-coded data to ASCII or IBM code; most such devices also convert speed as well. For instance, they accept Baudot-coded data at 75 baud and output ASCII data at 1200 bps. These units usually have considerable storage capabilities so that they can accept high-speed data for output at a lower speed. Such units with large solid-state memories often are used in place of paper tape devices. In the future, interface protocol converters are likely as well. Protocol converters, such as asynchronous to bisync, or bisync to SDLC, are now practical using microprocessors.

Other devices, such as multiplexers, concentrators, bridges, sharing units, and multiport modems, are dealt with in this book's companion volume, *Advanced Techniques in Data Communications.*

Ralph Glasgal is president of Glasgal Communications Services, manufacturers' representatives specializing in data communications equipment, with offices in Old Tappan, New Jersey, and covering the New York metropolitan area. Being affiliated with some of the most successful data communications equipment manufacturers and working closely with many of the leading corporate communications managers has given Mr. Glasgal an unusual opportunity to accumulate practical and broad-based systems design experience.

His many articles on data communications systems have appeared in Telecommunications, Datacom User, Electronics, *and* Signal *magazines.*

Mr. Glasgal completed his Engineering Physics studies at Cornell University in 1954 and acquired a Master's degree in Electrical Engineering at New York University in 1962. His work with RCA, Siemens, and Comfax has provided him with a diversified background in modems, terminals, memories, and digital data transmission systems.

In recognition of his exploration and scientific activities as chief auroral physicist at Wilkes Station in the Antarctic during the International Geophysical Year, Glasgal Island has been named for him.